# Windows™ 3.0: A Definitive Guide for DOS Users

# Windows™ 3.0: A Definitive Guide for DOS Users

Michael Vose

**Addison-Wesley Publishing Company, Inc.**
Reading, Massachusetts Menlo Park, California New York
Don Mills, Ontario Wokingham, England Amsterdam Bonn Sydney
Singapore Tokyo Madrid San Juan

ISBN: 0-201-55030-X



Production Editor: Amorette Pedersen
Cover design by Mark Sylvester/Skolos, Wedell + Raynor, Inc.
Set in 11-point Palatino by Benchmark Productions

ABCDEFGHIJ-MW-943210
First Printing, June 1990

# *Acknowledgments*

I would like to extend my personal thanks to my business partner Stan Miastkowski for his support during the writing of this book. My appreciation also goes out to my parents for their encouragement, and to my son Cary and wife Louise for putting up with my crazy schedule during the book's creation.

On a professional level, I offer my thanks to Claudette Moore for her skillful handling of contractual matters, and for her hours on the phone providing moral support. The sterling staff at Benchmark Productions—Chris Williams, who conceived of this book, and editors Amorette Pedersen and Allison Cox—deserve my kudos, as well.

Finally, I offer my thanks to Ed Juge, Director of Market Planning at Tandy Corporation, for the loan of the Tandy 4000 computer system which I used to run Windows 3.0 during the preparation of the manuscript. I also appreciate the help I received from Anderson Consulting and Software (North Bonneville, WA) for their Tiffany Plus screen capture program.

*Michael Vose*
*Peterborough, NH*
*May, 1990*

# Table of Contents

# *Introduction*

## About This Book

This book explains how to make Microsoft Windows work. It assumes (but does not require) that you have a working knowledge of DOS, and want to apply what you know toward understanding Windows. Knowing DOS makes Windows easier to learn. Learning Windows makes DOS easier to use. If you don't know DOS very well, you can still use this book to learn Windows. In the process, you might learn how to use your computer for tasks you didn't even know were possible.

The book is divided into two sections. Section One is mostly about Windows: how to install it, get it running, navigate its graphical user interface, modify its look and feel with the Control Panel, and use its accessories. Section Two is a survival guide for DOS users: it explains how to perform all the tasks under Windows you used to do with DOS, including maintaining disks, directories, and files. This section also explains the relationship between Windows and DOS configuration files.

Since Windows comes with an impressive instruction manual—and even an extensive on-line "manual"—why would you need a book like this one?

Manuals need to tell you everything you ever wanted to know (and many things you didn't) about a piece of software. But most people just want to make a program work. This book will help you understand how to make Windows work without forcing you to soak up every detail about its design. Once you learn the important and fundamental concepts that make Windows work, you can go back and refine your knowledge by examining its subtleties. This book can help you make it work and learn the important subtleties when and where they are most helpful.

### *Finding Your Way*

This book's topics are organized according to the way most people will learn and use Windows. The first section contains eight chapters. Chapter One explains how DOS and Windows compare—their similarities and differences. Chapter Two walks through Windows installation. Chapter Three explores the different modes Windows 3.0 runs in, some compatibility issues regarding the various versions of Windows, and the basic skills for using Windows. Chapter Four provides a get-acquainted tour of Windows. Chapter Five will get you started using Windows and its many accessories. Chapter Six gives you suggestions for modifying the look and feel of Windows. Chapter Eight explores how application programs and Windows interact.

Section Two contains four chapters. Chapter Nine explains how to use Windows to perform the classic DOS tasks for maintaining disks and files. Chapter Ten provides tips on using Windows and DOS together to tackle more serious disk-related tasks. Chapter 11 delves into the way Windows and various hardware components affect each other. Chapter 12 explains how Windows deals with TSRs and networks.

### *Conventions*

Any information that you might have to type on a keyboard appears in this book in a different typeface. These entries look like this:

```
device=ega.sys
```

Anytime you see the abbreviations for keyboard keys with a plus (+) sign between them, you should press and hold the first key and then press the second one.

With these conventions in mind, enjoy your foray into the world of Windows 3.0.

## A Brief History of Windows

You do not need to understand the historical and technical factors behind Windows 3.0 to use it successfully. If you are not interested in these issues, move ahead to Chapter 1 to get started using Windows 3.0.

The point-and-shoot, visually-oriented user interface, pioneered on Apple's Lisa and Macintosh, has come to be seen as a way to protect users from an operating system's cryptic command line. With over 20 years of human factors research behind it, the graphical user interface can make using a computer easier for users of all skill levels. When announced to the world in November of 1983, Microsoft Windows was touted as the Macintosh-like graphical user interface for DOS. Finally delivered in the fall of 1985, Windows was too big and too slow for most of the machines then available to run it, and there were few applications that used it. Instead of being a part of DOS, Windows was used like a DOS application. Since then, Windows, DOS, and Intel microprocessor-based machines have come a long way.

### *The Windows-DOS Connection*

DOS stands for Disk Operating System, but DOS manages many other computer resources beside floppy and fixed disks. DOS functions as part of a layer of software and helps manage an application program's interactions with the keyboard, video screen, serial and parallel ports, and specialized devices plugged into the computer's expansion bus. DOS provides a way for programmers to exploit the interrupt-driven design of the computer's microprocessor. Having this kind of control of the computer's hardware through a standard software layer like DOS lets programmers write applications that fully exploit the hardware to allow users to be as productive as possible.

Most of us do not need to understand how DOS controls the computer's underlying hardware. The part of DOS that most of us use is the *command interpreter*, the DOS module that interprets commands typed at the keyboard. DOS users are already familiar with this command interpreter, which is stored on the computer's boot-up disk as COMMAND.COM. The command interpreter's prompt is the ubiquitous C> or A>. From this prompt, you can type a number of commands to handle disk files or set up your hardware.

Windows does away with the command-line interface and replaces it with a graphical user interface (GUI). A GUI speeds up your day-to-day work with a computer by doing away with chores like typing disk drive, directory, and filenames on the keyboard. Windows 3.0 also lets a computer run many programs at the same time.

### Windows: Not the New Kid on the Block

Although Windows has been around since 1985, the vast majority of PC users ignored it until recently. Windows early on gained a reputation for poor performance. Recognizing this liability, software developers did not rush to create applications that exploited the Windows graphical user interface. People who really needed a graphical user interface often bought a Macintosh.

The main reason for this Windows disdain had little to do with Windows itself: the problem was the Intel microprocessor's restrictions on memory use. DOS runs in the 80x86 chip's Real mode and can only make 640K bytes of memory available to the operating system and its applications. Because it is a large program, Windows runs poorly in Real mode. It must constantly swap parts of itself to disk to make room in memory for application code and data. This problem becomes especially acute when more than one Windows application is running. Even the use of expanded memory under the Lotus/Intel/Microsoft Expanded Memory Specification (EMS) couldn't make Windows perform satisfactorily, partly because bank switching of memory is itself a sluggish process. Windows/386 ran acceptably due to the speed of 80386 chips and the ability to run several separate sessions of DOS and Windows, each with its own 640K of memory.

The IBM/Microsoft solution to this dilemma was OS/2, an operating system that had a graphical user interface and ran in the Intel chip's Protected mode. Protected mode opens up memory addressing to 16 megabytes and up, moving from the 80286 to the 80386 and beyond. Protected mode also offers memory protection mechanisms to prevent a single errant program from bringing the computer down when multiple programs were running.

But while IBM/Microsoft struggled to get a usable version of OS/2 off the drawing board, numerous software vendors began using something called a DOS Extender to run DOS programs in Protected mode on 80286-and-up processors. DOS Extender code was built into an application to let programs use the larger and faster extended memory of Intel processors remaining DOS-compatible. A DOS Extender provides DOS-compatibility by using a mechanism to switch the microprocessor back into Real mode any time a program needs to perform a DOS-controlled function. When DOS is done, the DOS Extender switches the processor back into Protected mode and resumes operation of the application program.

Microsoft decided to add DOS-extender technology to Windows to improve its performance by letting more of the Windows code reside in memory. Windows 3.0 adds together all free conventional memory and all installed extended memory into one contiguous memory area for running its own code and applications. This technology provides the added bonus of allowing Windows applications to be larger than under previous versions, and to use the protection mechanisms of the microprocessor's Protected mode to keep multiple programs in memory from conflicting with one another.

Windows 3.0 with its built-in DOS-extender gives application developers a single target for developing programs to exploit Protected mode. For users, this single target will mean that more applications can be written to use the Windows' graphical user interface without fear of degrading performance. In addition, programs that need more memory can now take advantage of the large memory afforded by Protected mode.

### A New Era

Windows 3.0 brings a new era to DOS computing. Just two years ago, many people were predicting the demise of DOS, the end of the DOS era. Windows 3.0 gives new life to the DOS era by making DOS work better.

In the pages that follow, you will learn how Windows 3.0 can make you work better, too.

# PART ONE

# *Windows—A Super Shell for DOS*

# CHAPTER 1

# *Windows and DOS*

Windows is a DOS companion program that was written to make DOS more accessible for everyday use. Windows provides a new way to work with DOS. It gives DOS a new look and makes working with a computer's disks, files, and applications easier. Windows uses a graphical user interface, and it lets you run more than one program at the same time. Windows 3.0 breaks the DOS 640K memory barrier and lets Windows applications use as much memory as a computer can hold. Also, Windows provides a common look and feel for all of a computer's applications.

Windows is not an operating system, it is an operating environment that sits on top of DOS. DOS remains the underlying control program for the computer. Windows provides many new functions that DOS cannot perform. Windows offers a friendlier, more attractive way to interact with both DOS and a personal computer.

This chapter explains how DOS and Windows compare to each other, and how Windows relates to a genre of programs called DOS Shells.

## How DOS and Windows Are Alike

Both DOS and Windows perform the basic operations essential to using your computer effectively. These operations include loading and running application programs, managing your disks and files, and adapting new hardware components to your machine. Usually, when you perform an operation under Windows, it is simply executing a DOS command or equivalent for you.

Like DOS, Windows lets you start, run, and leave applications. Windows can print files in the background like the DOS Spool command. Windows can set and use DOS internal system values like Date and Time. Windows can create a DOS system disk. Windows can control communications ports. Windows displays disk directories with the same (and sometimes greater than) flexibility as DOS. Windows can display the contents of a file. Windows can show a graphical representation of a directory tree.

Windows lets you format and label disks; create and destroy directories; copy, delete, and move files; and print files. While DOS requires a separate utility to locate files on a disk, Windows has a built-in command for this purpose. After it finds a file you asked it to search for, Windows reports the exact location of that file regardless of its drive or subdirectory location. Windows also has a built-in mechanism for changing a file's attributes. Unlike DOS, these operations can be done without typing commands; you supply just an occasional name for a new file or directory, or a search key.

Windows and DOS both have a core program module, called the *kernel*, that stays in memory whenever the computer is running. Your applications programs call on the Windows kernel when they need its services, and on the DOS kernel for its services. Virtually anything you can do under DOS you can do with Windows—often with far less hassle!

## How DOS and Windows Are Different

Even though DOS and Windows are fundamentally alike and have the same basic purpose, there are still some substantial differences between them. These differences mainly revolve around the different duties each was designed to perform.

DOS provides low-level control over hardware. This low-level control is seldom important to the user of a DOS program. The DOS services used by an application program are invoked by the program itself. Users of programs do not have to tell DOS to open a disk file for data input or output (I/O); programmers tell DOS to do these operations when they write the program. You can control certain kinds of hardware from DOS; for example, the DOS command MODE lets you switch from color to monochrome video modes.

In contrast, Windows offers high-level control of the interaction between the computer and its user. While Windows gives you an easy way to communicate with DOS, it usually leaves the actual management of the computer's hardware up to DOS. Windows provides a Control Panel (explained in detail in Chapter 6) that lets you change certain hardware settings. Windows then sends this new information to DOS (or sometimes directly to the hardware) to make the changes you want.

### *The Graphical User Interface*

The most obvious new capability Windows offers is its graphical user interface (GUI) and desktop workspace. When Windows starts running, it creates a graphical representation of a desktop on your computer's screen. Figure 1-1 shows the desktop users will find when they load Windows for the first time. The components of the GUI include windows and menus that pop open and present options and dialog boxes that prompt you for information.

*Figure 1-1: The Windows desktop upon loading.*

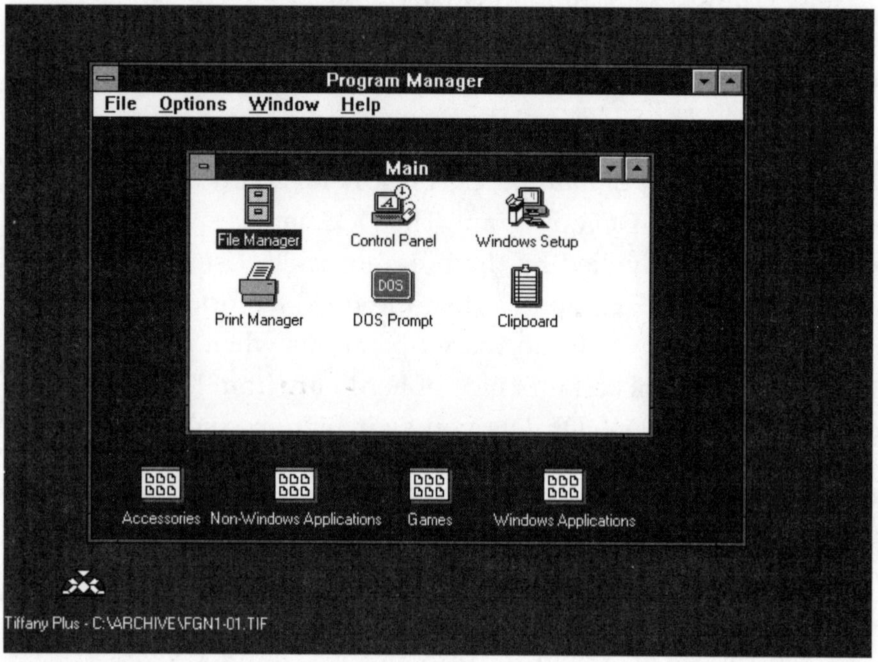


From the Windows desktop, you can "open" file drawers and read letters and other documents; you can set aside a document and start using a calculator or spreadsheet while having the first document you worked with still at your side. You can print a letter and then immediately start working on a different project while the print job finishes. If you get a phone call and need to look something up to answer the caller's question, you can just open or switch to another application and quickly retrieve the information you need.

The graphical look of Windows gives all of the programs designed to run under it a more consistent appearance. Besides looking comfortably familiar, these programs will all perform routine operations, like retrieving a file, *in the same way*. Windows programs all use similar pull-down menus to make available the variety of operations the application offers.

This similarity in the look and feel of Windows programs makes it easier to learn other Windows programs once you've learned your first one.

### *Visual Modes, Icons, and Screen Fonts*

The most immediately noticeable difference between DOS and Windows is the change from a character-based to a graphics screen. Character-based screens use a single font for all displayed characters. They cannot display italic or bold letters and numbers on the screen; they can only indicate italic, bold, and underlined text by using attributes like reverse video, or by using color to identify italic or underlined text.

Using a screen's graphics mode, however, allows the use of finely-detailed graphics images. Windows uses many kinds of graphic images including symbols called icons. Icons can represent programs or data files. For example, the icon for Write, the Windows word processor, is a pencil (see Figure 1-2). You can move icons around on the screen and even use them to start an application running. Once it is running, you can clear an application off your desktop temporarily by shrinking it back to an icon. Running applications that have been minimized to icons appear at the bottom of the desktop screen in an icon area.

*Figure 1-2: The icon for the Windows word processor, Write.*

Graphics screens also make possible the use of different character fonts for letters and numbers, and proportional character spacing. Mixing fonts on a screen lets you see italics and bold letters and words along with normal text. A graphical display lets you see work in the way it will appear when you print it on one of today's high-resolution laser printers or a plotter.

In character-based screens, you cannot have multiple fonts (fonts are a style of typeface, such as Helvetica) on the screen at one time. Often you are not able to see the fonts you've chosen properly displayed. Because everything under Windows is graphics-based, you can see all the different fonts, as well as italicized and bold type.

Figure 1-3 shows a Windows desktop that displays the icons of 18 simultaneously running applications or accessories. Placing the mouse pointer over any one of these icons and clicking the mouse button twice will reactivate that program. Each running program under Windows is called a *task*.

*Figure 1-3: Minimized icons of programs running at the same time.*

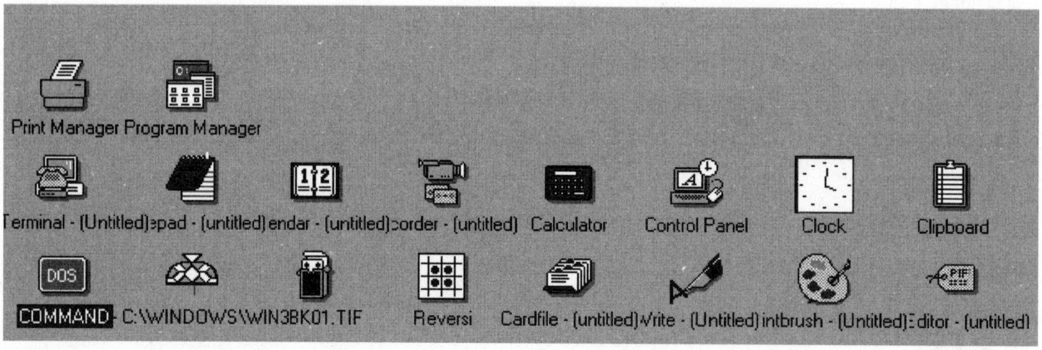


### Event-Driven Versus Procedural Programs

Windows and the applications written to use it subtly alter the way a user interacts with a computer. Under Windows, a program becomes strictly event-driven rather than procedural.

Using an event-driven program compares to using a traditional procedural one the way driving a car compares to riding a bus. The driver controls where the car goes while a bus passenger goes only where the bus can take him and only on the buses' schedule. Event-driven programs are 80 percent interactive and 20 percent processing oriented while traditional programs tend to be 20 percent interactive and 80 percent processing oriented.

Procedural programs perform all their actions in a preset order. These programs may offer a menu of choices for different operations like "Print Report," but once you choose a certain operation, the program performs its actions one after another and you cannot alter that order. When entering data into a program written this way, you often have to start over if you make a mistake somewhere along the way.

An event-driven program turns this scheme around and lets the user pick what happens next during a program's run. Users choose *when* an event happens. To make such a choice, a user sends a message to Windows to perform some action. Windows is always ready to receive these messages; they stack up in a message queue so that a message never gets lost. A user can choose to print a report at any time, even during the middle of some other operation. When the user chooses "Print," usually from a pull-down menu, Windows gets the message and responds immediately.

As a result of this subtle change in user/computer interaction, DOS users must slightly alter their thinking about how to execute an action. Under DOS, copying a file requires you to issue a command followed by a filename. For example, the DOS command

```
copy c:myfile.txt a:myfile.bak
```

copies the file named MYFILE.TXT located on drive C: to a floppy disk in drive A: and gives it the name MYFILE.BAK.

Under Windows, you first choose the files you want to copy by highlighting them on the screen. Then, you choose the Copy option from a File menu (see Figure 1-4) and you will be met by a dialog box like the one shown in Figure 1-5 to actually copy the file. This reverses the way you interact with DOS: you identify an object, like a file or a line of text, and tell the program what event you want to happen to that object. Chapter 9 deals with the subject of files and directories in depth.

*Figure 1-4: A File menu.*

### The Mouse and the Command Line

Another substantial difference between DOS and Windows is its preferential use of a mouse over the keyboard to enter commands. Since most actions the computer can perform have a visual representation (an icon) on a Windows screen, pointing at that visual object becomes the primary way to interact with the machine. You can still use the keyboard as a pointing device using the arrow keys to "point" the cursor at a screen object. A mouse will be faster, however, and offer finer control over the movement of the pointer than cursor keys can provide for a cursor.

(Under Windows, a mouse controls a screen pointer that looks like an arrowhead, while the keyboard controls the movement of a more traditional cursor, which frequently takes the shape of a highlight bar.) Later chapters in this book will explain how combining the actions of a mouse with the keyboard yield the best productivity when using Windows.

*Figure 1-5: The Copy option dialog box.*

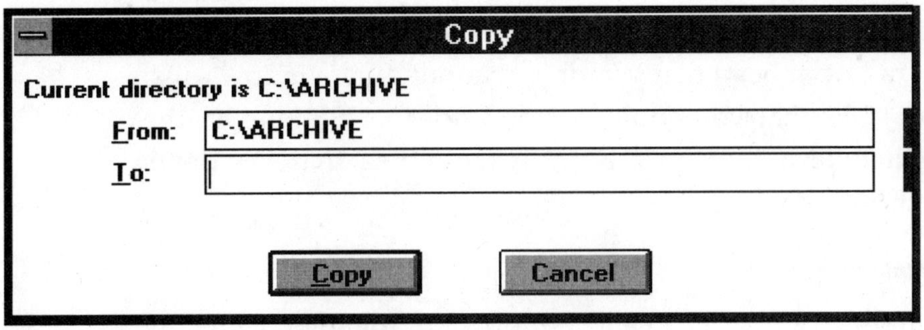


### *Device Independence*

Since Windows is a layer through which all programs interact with the computer, Windows can provide device independence to application software. Windows deals with devices like printers and video adapters so that individual applications do not have to provide that support. Programs written to run under Windows can use any hardware that itself has been adapted for Windows. Printer manufacturers need only write a Windows printer driver to work with any and all Windows application programs. Individual applications no longer have to supply a disk full of printer or other device drivers.

### *Multitasking*

Windows manages the computer's memory so you can run more than one application at a time. This capability is called *multitasking*. With multitasking, there is no real limit to the number of applications you can open. If Windows runs out of memory, it swaps data and code to disk using either swap files or, on 80386 computers, a process called *virtual memory*. This swapping leaves room in memory for another application to run; you really don't need to be aware of this process, it all happens automatically.

As you can see, the differences between DOS and Windows are quite complementary as you might expect since they come from the same company. Windows lets you issue DOS commands or perform standard DOS operations without typing commands. DOS is always available to let you perform any task (a few at best) that Windows cannot. But Windows also lets you do many tasks that you could not do under DOS alone. In the next section, we'll take a look at the *new* capabilities that Windows brings to your computer interactions.

### Windows Brings New Capabilities

With an understanding of how DOS and Windows fit together, let's now look at what Windows allows you to do that DOS will not. The features of Windows go far beyond just making DOS easier to work with. The Windows graphical user interface provides a significantly improved way of interacting with a computer. Windows can help novices quickly learn to use a computer, but it also can make a knowledgeable user more productive day-by-day by letting the computer work more the way you do. The following Windows features will help get more from your computer.

**The Task Manager** People seldom do only one job at a time, so Windows lets you perform more than one computer task at a time. Windows lets you switch back and forth among applications, regardless of the number of programs running. The *Task Manager*, a window that lists all currently running tasks (see Figure 1-6), lets you scroll among tasks and choose the one you want to switch to. Pressing Enter or clicking on the Switch To button immediately makes that program active. If the program had previously been minimized to an icon, switching to it makes it active again and redisplays it on the screen.

*Figure 1-6: The Task Manager.*

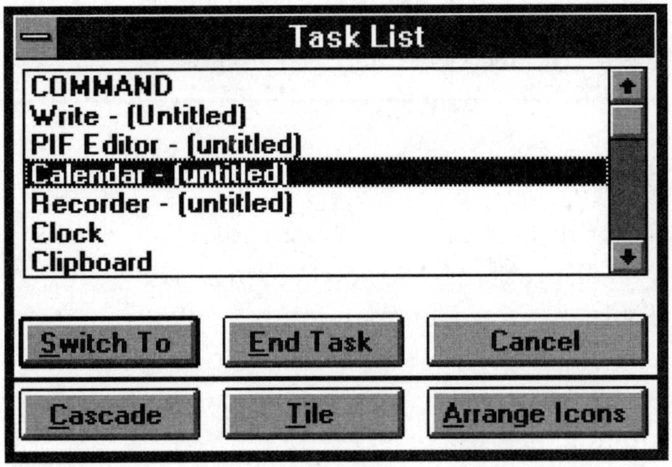


**The Clipboard** Windows also has built-in mechanisms to permit moving data from one application to another. Using an accessory called the *Clipboard*, you can copy text or graphics from one application to another. Under DOS, copying or moving data between applications would involve using intermediate files and many separate data-transfer steps.

**Accessories** Because Windows can run many programs at once, Windows creators have provided a number of accessories with the environment. These accessory programs give you instant access to some productivity tools that you would otherwise have to buy separately. The accessories include a calculator, a notepad, a mini word processor, a calendar, a clock, a keystroke recorder, an index-card filer, a telecommunications/terminal program, and a paint program. With these accessory applications alone, your computer running Windows can be a productivity powerhouse. We'll explore the accessories in more detail in Chapter 5.

**The Help System** An often-overlooked feature of Windows—sorely missing from DOS—is a help system that you can open on your screen anytime you run into trouble. Pressing the F1 key or using the Help pull-down menu lets you call up an on-line manual that will give you information about how to perform any Windows operation. The Help menus offer several categories of information so that hunting around through multiple screens to find what you need isn't necessary. There is even a help screen that explains how to use the help system.

## How DOS Shells and Windows Compare

DOS shells are programs that attempt to make DOS easier to use. The names of the many popular DOS shell programs—Disc Director, 1 Dir Plus, Q-DOS II, Xtree DOS, PC Tools, Norton Commander, Magellan, and others—may be familiar to you. With version 4.0, DOS itself even comes with a shell called the MS-DOS Shell. DOS shells proliferate because so many people want to streamline their use of DOS.

DOS shells surround DOS and attempt to fill in the functional gaps that keep DOS from being as useful as it could be. Shells also try to make DOS look less intimidating by displaying disk directory tree diagrams and lists of files in neat little boxes instead of a mostly blank screen with its insistent flashing cursor beside the nondescript C> prompt. DOS shells make file management easier by assigning DOS commands to function keys and by letting you tag (or select) files for copying or other operations. In their most recent incarnations, DOS shells provide a file viewing capability that lets you examine a file in its native format without loading the application that created the file. DOS shells often support a mouse, and most provide menus from which you can launch applications. DOS shells provide a semi-graphical user interface in that they divide the screen up into boxed areas that are similar to windows and often use pull-down menus. These user-interfaces use the computer's character mode, however, not its graphic mode. This restricts displays to the use of just one font and limits the colors of the display.

How do Windows and DOS shells compare? In many ways, Windows *is* a DOS shell. It provides a rich set of file management tools and it lets you launch applications from a central location. But while shells offer little more than these features, Windows goes far beyond them.

Windows is more of an environment than a mere DOS shell. The file management tools built into Windows form just a small part of the environment. The built-in accessories that Windows provides make it a multivariant, integrated application that can perform many different jobs with just the click of a mouse button. Windows also provides a simple mechanism—the Clipboard—for sharing data among applications.

Windows' relationship to applications is a key difference between Windows and DOS shells. As much as it is a shell for DOS, Windows is also a shell for applications because it allows programs to be written to use the same user-interface components as Windows itself. Using these components, Windows applications have a consistent appearance and operate similarly enough that a user can become proficient with a new application in just a short time.

Most importantly, Windows provides true multitasking on a DOS platform. You can run many Windows or non-Windows programs at the same time. The more memory you add to the computer, the more programs you can run at once. You can switch back and forth among applications with ease and an application can continue to run in the background while you work with another application in the foreground. This ability to run many programs at once means, for example, that your computer can monitor on-line communications services and receive e-mail or stock quotes while you write letters or extract information from a database. The advantages of multitasking are many.

With an 80386-based computer, Windows can even run non-Windows applications inside their own window, and can use the Clipboard to exchange data with these applications and almost any other application. Windows gives you a multitude of ways to control how non-Windows programs interact with other applications and Windows itself.

Windows can rightly be called a super-shell because it provides functions that DOS does not have, while making traditional DOS tasks easier. Additionally, Windows gives DOS multitasking capability and a way to exchange data among applications.

### The Migration Path

Windows makes a computer more like a workstation than an earlier-generation personal computer. In this role, Windows can equip users to cope with the environments they are likely to encounter on tomorrow's machines.

Windows follows a set of guidelines for user interfaces called Systems Application Architecture (SAA). These IBM-developed guidelines, called Common User Access, are also the foundation for OS/2 Presentation Manager and all the other operating systems/environments that will eventually comply with SAA. Using Windows 3.0 can help you learn a method of interacting with computers that will become increasingly widespread. This method will someday span hardware platforms from workstations to mainframes.

Using Windows today will make adapting to Presentation Manager virtually painless. Windows 3.0 and Presentation Manager exhibit only minor differences. Users who find themselves working in an office that uses both Windows and OS/2-based computers will not have to make adjustments when switching from one machine to another.

Furthermore, Microsoft has stated that OS/2 version 2.0, which is slated for delivery in late 1990, will provide a layer of code to allow Windows programs to run under the Presentation Manager, which will make it easy for developers to create Windows 3.0 programs that will run on both DOS and OS/2 machines.

## Summary

Windows and DOS have many similarities. They are both designed to let you use an Intel-based personal computer to run programs, manage disks and files, and send data to printers or other computers. The differences between DOS and Windows focus primarily on the added features that Windows provides to let you be more productive. Windows extends and complements DOS's capabilities.

The next chapter explains how to install Windows and how to start it running on your computer. It also shows you how to get the DOS prompt when you need to, and how to leave Windows. Chapter 3 provides some important information about the compatibility of the different versions of Windows, and an explanation of the modes in which Windows 3.0 runs. Chapter 3 closes with a discussion of the essential skills all Windows users will need to develop.

# CHAPTER 2

# *Installation and Setup*

Windows 3.0 comes with a program called Setup that automatically transfers Windows from its distribution disks to your computer and prepares it for operation. This installation program has two parts: a DOS portion and a Windows portion. Both parts run by themselves, but require occasional input from you.

You *must* use the Setup program to install Windows. Because Windows 3.0 is a large piece of software, all its files are distributed in compressed format to save disk space. These files must be decompressed before they can be copied and used. Setup does this job. You cannot copy files from the Windows distribution disks and just run Windows.

This chapter explains Windows installation and how to start Windows, exit to the DOS prompt, and leave Windows.

## Running Setup

Before you begin, **make sure you have at least 6 to 8 megabytes of free hard disk space**. To run the two-part Setup program, place Disk 1 of the Windows distribution disk set into a floppy disk drive on your computer. Make sure the drive you put the disk into is active by typing its letter designation followed by a colon. Then, type

```
setup <ENTER>
```

and follow the instructions on the screen.

When you see the initial Windows Setup screen, and anytime during installation, you can press F1 for help in using Setup. You can also exit Setup at any time by pressing F3. If you do leave Setup before it finishes its work, Windows 3.0 will not be properly installed on your computer. You will need to run Setup again to complete the installation.

After the initial "Welcome to Setup" screen, the installation program asks a series of questions over the next several screens. Each of these questions appears above a box that you can type into to answer a question. There will be text in reverse video in the box already—this is the Setup program's default answer for any given question. To accept the default answer, just press Enter. Windows will automatically detect what computer you use, what display, what mouse, keyboard, keyboard layout (U.S.), language, and whether or not the computer is hooked to a network.

Keep in mind the following points when installing Windows:

- If an earlier version of Windows is already running on your system and for some reason you want to keep it there, be sure to specify a different directory name for Windows 3.0.
- Some monitors have drivers that you must install according to the manufacturer's specification. If Windows' Setup does not specify your monitor, check the monitor documentation for information specific to installation with Windows.
- After you have made these initial choices, Windows will install several files and prompt you for another disk. You then go into a Windows management screen called Setup, at which point you

make your printer and application choices. Be prepared to tell Setup what printer you use.
- You can always get help by pressing F1.

If you're not sure about an answer, you can usually accept what Windows offers as a default and that will work fine. For example, if you don't remember what brand of mouse you are using, accept the choice made by Setup. If it proves to be the wrong choice, you can run Setup again later to change mouse choices.

Once you have made the necessary choices for the DOS portion of Setup, the installation program copies a series of files onto your hard disk. Then, it loads and runs the Windows portion of the Setup operation. This part of Setup runs Windows itself.

This will likely be your first experience with Windows. The first thing you will notice is that most text now appears inside individual windows on the screen. You will also notice that the text inside those windows looks different; in fact, Windows now displays text using its own character set instead of the character set that comes with your computer. Windows draws these characters using the computer's graphics capability and can display letters in a variety of character sets, or *fonts*. You will also notice that many of the windows you see on your screen have buttons and other controls associated with them. You can now manipulate those controls with your mouse, or the keyboard if your computer does not use a mouse. The section "Starting Windows," later in this chapter, explains how to start interacting with Windows.

### The CONFIG.SYS and AUTOEXEC.BAT Files

One of the last things the Windows portion of Setup does is to modify your CONFIG.SYS and AUTOEXEC.BAT files. If you do not understand how these system files affect your computer, just accept the Setup program's default actions. Otherwise, you can elect to review and edit the changes before Setup makes them. You can also choose to wait and make these modifications yourself at a later date.

The CONFIG.SYS and AUTOEXEC.BAT files provide information your computer uses upon startup to configure itself. Later chapters in this book discuss in more detail how Windows uses these files.

One change Setup may *not* make to AUTOEXEC.BAT is to add the root directory to the directory search path. Without the root directory in the search path, Windows gives you an error message box that tells you it cannot find the DOS command interpreter, COMMAND.COM, when you click on the DOS Prompt icon in the Windows Program Manager Main applications group (more on this group later). If you feel comfortable doing so, you should use a text editor like the Windows Notepad or the Write accessory to make this change to AUTOEXEC.BAT before you reboot after installing Windows. Make sure the PATH statement looks something like this:

```
PATH=C:\;C:\WINDOWS
```

If you plan to use Windows exclusively—and most people will—you should also add

```
win
```

as the last line in your AUTOEXEC batch file. This "command," which is the filename of the Windows' kernel executable file, will automatically run Windows whenever you start or reboot your computer.

Finally, Setup runs a printer installation module. You will be asked to scroll through a long list of printers and choose the printer you use with your computer. When you finish printer installation, Setup prompts you to reboot your computer.

Now, you are ready to find out what Windows is all about. Before moving on to learn how Windows operates, here is a final note about Setup.

You can use Setup to make changes to the Windows environment after installation; Chapter 7 explores how to make these modifications.

During the whirlwind introduction to Windows that follows, you'll learn how to enter and exit Windows and how to get to the DOS prompt any time you need to.

## Starting Windows

Getting in and out of Windows is easy. The simplest way to start Windows is to add a line to your AUTOEXEC.BAT file, as explained previously, so that Windows loads automatically when you turn on your computer. But you can also load Windows by typing its name at the DOS prompt.

Loading a program under DOS merely involves entering the program's name, and Windows is no exception. The program name for Windows is "win." To load Windows from the DOS prompt, simply type

```
win<ENTER>
```

As detailed in the next chapter, you can load Windows in one of three different modes; to load Windows in Real mode, type

```
win /r<ENTER>
```

or you can replace the "/r" with "/s" or "/3" to load Windows in either of its other modes.

Since there may be times when you want to run an older version application under Windows 3.0, you will occasionally need to run Windows in Real mode. If you previously started Windows automatically—undoubtedly in Protected mode—you will need to exit Windows and restart it in Real mode. (If you can never be certain from one day to the next in which mode you will need to be, load Windows from the DOS prompt and do not put the "win" line in your AUTOEXEC.BAT file.)

Before looking at how to exit Windows, let's see how to make a quick escape to DOS.

### Returning to the DOS Prompt

Since you know DOS better than Windows at the moment, you might want to see that familiar C> prompt in case you get frustrated with Windows. There are two ways to return to the DOS prompt. One way is to leave Windows, as explained in the next section. The other is to use Windows itself to get to the DOS prompt.

When Windows loads, it starts a task called the Program Manager and displays this desktop control accessory in a window in the middle of the screen. Within the Program Manager window, you will see icons that represent application groups. When you first install Windows, there are anywhere from three to five application groups in the Program Manager window: the Accessory, Main, and Games groups, plus Windows and non-Windows application groups. You can open any of these group windows to view icons that represent the utilities that come with Windows and the applications installed on your computer.

When you choose the Main application group by double clicking the mouse with the screen pointer at the Main group icon, a window opens to display six other icons that represent Windows' essential tasks (see Figure 2-1). One of those icons, appropriately labeled DOS Prompt, lets you jump out of Windows to the DOS prompt. Choose the DOS Prompt icon with your mouse, or use your keyboard arrow keys to move the blue highlight bar to the words "DOS Prompt" below the icon and press Enter to jump to DOS. This action takes you to that old friend, the C> prompt. To return to Windows, press Crtl+Esc to bring up the Task Manager, as explained in Chapter 1. The Task Manager makes it easy to switch back to the Program Manager task by selecting the Switch To button (make sure the Program Manager is the highlighted task); this action brings you back into Windows while leaving the DOS Prompt task active. Alternatively, you can type "exit" at the DOS prompt to close the DOS task and return to Windows.

DOS veterans will recognize that Windows uses the shell facility to start the DOS Prompt task. This facility is used by many application programs to allow a user to jump temporarily to DOS without leaving the application.

*Figure 2-1: Icons representing Windows' essential tasks.*

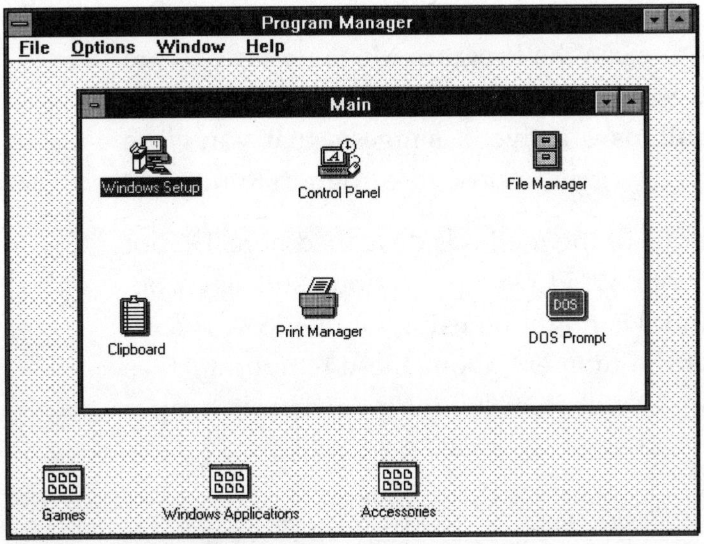


### *Quitting Windows*

Getting out of Windows when you need to is also simple, although it may require a few steps. Windows can run many programs at once and each one is called an *active task*. Before you can exit Windows, you first have to close all active tasks, whether they are applications, running accessories, or Windows program-control managers such as the File Manager or the Print Manager. To close a task, you first pull down its *Control menu* (one click with the mouse on the miniature spacebar icon in the upper-left corner of the window, or press Alt+Spacebar) and select the

Close option. Alternatively, you can double click on the Control menu icon with your mouse to exit a task, or press Alt+F4 to select Close while bypassing the menu. If you had previously started a DOS Prompt task, you can exit that task by returning to the C> prompt and typing "exit" followed by Enter.

When all active tasks are closed, you can then exit Windows by selecting the Program Manager's Control menu and choosing the Close option. Alternately, you can choose the Program Manager's File menu and choose the option, Exit Windows (see Figure 2-2). In other words, the Program Manager task in the last task you close; by closing that task, you exit Windows. If you try to close the Program Manager task before you've closed all the other active tasks, Windows displays a message box that explains that there are still tasks active; it suggests that you close those active tasks first and then try again to close the Program Manager.

Always leave Windows using one of the methods described here. Do not just turn your computer off with Windows applications still open because any temporary files Windows might be using will be lost. You do not need to know anything at the moment about these temporary files except that they exist. Chapter 10 discusses how Windows uses temporary files.

*Figure 2-2: The Program Manager's file menu.*

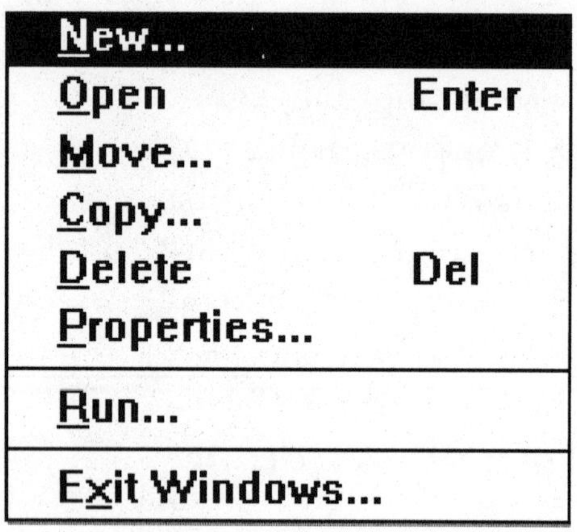

## Summary

Windows uses the Setup utility to install itself automatically. You have to provide the answers to a few simple questions about what disks and directories you want Windows to use. Once it is installed, starting Windows, moving to the DOS prompt, and leaving Windows are all simple operations.

This chapter introduced several terms and ideas about Windows that you may not yet fully understand. The next chapter explains the different modes that Windows runs in, and explores the essential skills you will need to become proficient using Windows.

# CHAPTER 3

# *Windows Essentials*

Windows 3.0 brings new features and capabilities to IBM PC-compatible computers. The most important of these new features is built-in DOS Extender technology that allows applications to address all the available memory in your machine. While you do not need to know about extended memory, to run Windows you should be aware of the compatibility issues between version 3.0 and earlier versions of Windows.

Unlike its earlier versions, Windows 3.0 also runs in several different modes depending upon the hardware of the computer.

To use Windows, you need to acquire only a few new skills: how to use a mouse, interact with windows and menus, and switch among multiple tasks. Once you have mastered these basics, working with Windows becomes second nature.

## The Different Versions of Windows

The first two major versions of Windows—versions 1.x and 2.x—ran exclusively in the Real mode of Intel 80x86 microprocessors. Application programs written for either of these Windows versions were largely compatible with each other. Windows version 2.x supplanted version 1.x and the latter is no longer offered by Microsoft. Windows version 2.x will also eventually be replaced by Windows 3.0. Table 3-1 summarizes the relationships among the various versions of Windows.

*Table 3-1: Compatibility among Windows' versions.*

| | *MODE* | | |
|---|---|---|---|
| *Version* | *Real* | *Protected* | *Applications' Upward Compatibility Through Version 3.0* |
| Windows 1.x | Yes | No | Real mode only. |
| Windows 2.x | Yes | No | Real mode only. |
| Windows/386 | Yes | No | Real mode only. |
| Windows 3.0 | Yes | Yes | Real mode only. |

Windows 3.0 was redesigned from the ground up to exploit an AT-compatible's Protected mode, but it will also run in Real mode.

The 80286/386/486 processor's Protected mode provides hardware protection mechanisms that allow a computer to safely run many programs at once, and to allow the addressing of large amounts of memory. Real mode provides no protection mechanisms, which makes running more than one program at a time a risky undertaking. Real mode also restricts applications to using just 640K of memory.

Application programs written for Windows 3.0 will also run in either mode. Applications written for Windows version 2.x, however, will run under Windows 3.0 *only in Real mode*. This restriction is actually good news because it means that Windows 3.0 is backward compatible with version 2.x. You can use version 2.x applications under Windows 3.0, sacrificing Protected-mode capability. Any organization or individual that has an investment in Windows 2.x applications does not have to sacrifice that investment. Similarly, newcomers to Windows who need an application that is available only as a Windows 2.x program, can have access to that software. Windows 3.0 can run version 2.x programs that use expanded (EMS) memory, as well.

Windows version 2.x also exists in a special form for computers that use the 80386/486 microprocessor. Called Windows/386, this version also runs only in Real mode. The major difference between this and the 80286 version of Windows 2.x is its ability to run multiple 640K DOS sessions on a single 80386-based machine, provided that machine has sufficient memory. Windows/386 allows switching among these multiple DOS sessions similar to the way Windows allows switching among running tasks. Windows/386 applications also must run in Real mode under Windows 3.0.

## The Modes of Windows

The addition of DOS-extender technology to version 3.0 turns Windows into a *modal system,* one that has two or more modes. Most of us will never be aware that Windows 3.0 has three different modes because it automatically senses its hardware environment and loads in the mode appropriate for that hardware. But when you need to take advantage of the features of a different mode, you can run Windows 3.0 in any of the following modes (providing that you have the required hardware):

### Real Mode

Windows automatically starts up in Real mode on computers with less than 1 megabyte of memory. (On any machine that has less than 1 megabyte of memory, regardless of processor, Windows will start up in Real mode.) If you need to run applications written to work with Windows 2.x, you can start Windows 3.0 in Real mode on any machine by appending the "/r" switch to the **win** command (the command to launch Windows); you would type "win /r" at the DOS prompt. You can run Windows 3.0 in Real mode on any 80x86-based computer.

### Standard Mode

Windows starts up in Standard mode on any 80286-based computer, and on 80386/486 machines that have more than 1 megabyte but less than 2 megabytes of memory installed. Standard mode is Windows 3.0's normal operating mode. It provides access to extended memory which Windows uses to run multiple non-Windows applications. If you will not be using any non-Windows applications on an 80386/486 computer, Windows runs best in Standard mode, regardless of the amount of memory installed. To start Windows in Standard mode, you would type "win /s" at the DOS prompt.

### *386 Enhanced Mode*

Windows starts up in 386 Enhanced mode when your computer offers an 80386/486 processor and more than 2 megabytes of memory. This mode provides access to the 80386's virtual memory capability, which lets Windows applications use more memory than is physically available in the computer. In 386 Enhanced mode, non-Windows applications can be run in individual windows instead of full-screen (more on this subject in Chapter 8.) If you have an 80386 machine with between 1 and 2 megabytes of memory, you can start Windows in 386 Enhanced mode by typing "win /3" at the DOS prompt. Using such a machine in this mode will slow down the operation of Windows, but does provide access to virtual memory.

The performance of Windows is affected by its operating mode with the principal variable being the amount of memory installed in the computer. In Chapter 11, we will take a closer look at the different kinds of memory (conventional, extended, and expanded) available on DOS machines and explore how Windows' performance is affected by each.

You can find out what mode Windows is running in at any time by selecting the About option from the Help menu of either the Program or File Manager (see Figure 3-1).

*Figure 3-1: The About message box.*

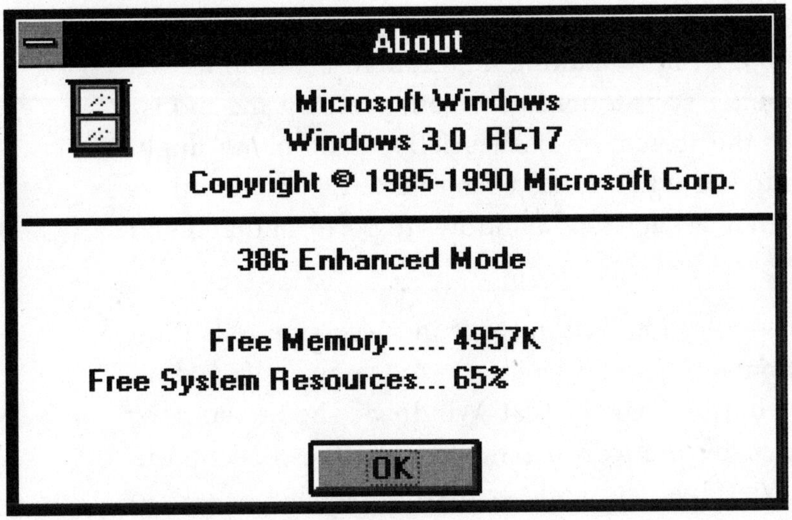


## Essential Windows Operations

The skills for efficiently using Windows break down into four major categories: mouse usage, window management, task switching, and menu manipulation. Mastering the techniques in these categories is all you need to succeed with Windows.

If you feel you have already mastered the basic techniques of using a mouse, moving and resizing windows, switching among tasks, and making choices from menus, you can skip the sections that follow and move along to the next chapter.

### *Mouse Operations*

A mouse is a hardware device for controlling a screen pointer. In Windows, the screen pointer is an arrowhead. When you move a mouse across the surface of a desk, the pointer on the screen moves as well. The pointer moves in the direction you move the mouse.

A mouse has from one to three buttons on it that you can push, an action more commonly called *clicking* because most mice make a clicking sound when you press a button. The mouse button lets you make the screen pointer perform an action, usually making a selection. For example, if you move the screen pointer so it touches an icon, pressing the mouse button selects that icon; the icon may flash briefly or its name might change to reverse video to show that it has been selected. For a menu selection, making a single mouse click tells Windows to perform that menu choice.

Quickly pressing a mouse selection button twice in succession tells Windows to begin some action. If the screen pointer is touching an icon, double-clicking the mouse button signals that Windows should start or resume the task identified by the icon. As the Control Panel section in Chapter 6 points out, Windows lets you set the double-click speed to match your personal preference.

A mouse can also be used to move a screen object. This process is called *dragging*. To move a window, you place the mouse pointer on the title bar, press and hold the mouse button down, and move the mouse in the direction you want to move the window. This action drags the window to a new location. Similarly, moving an icon simply involves dragging the icon to a new location. If you try to drag an object to a location that Windows does not permit, the screen pointer will change shape to a circle with a line through it (the international symbol for "no") to indicate that the movement is illegal.

Dragging can be useful for more than cosmetic reasons. The Windows File Manager lets you move files from one directory to another by dragging a file icon from one document window to another. Making the data in two separate windows visible simultaneously might give you a better view on a problem; moving those windows around will probably be necessary to get that view.

Resizing windows makes use of dragging too, in a slightly different way. The action is the same—press and hold the mouse button while moving the mouse—but the pointer looks different. Instead of an arrowhead, the pointer becomes a pair of arrowheads pointing in opposite directions. Only when you see this pointer can you drag a window border to enlarge or reduce the size of a window.

### *Window Management*

To control the placement and size of windows on the desktop, Windows provides these user-controllable functions: opening and closing, moving, cascading, tiling, and resizing windows.

Starting an application opens a window, places that window on top of any other open windows, and colors the title bar to show that the window is *active*. The active window is the one where all subsequent activity takes place until you move to a different window.

You can move from an active window to an inactive one by placing the screen pointer on any visible part of the inactive window and clicking the mouse button. This action will bring the inactive window to the foreground and change the color of its title bar to show that it is now active. If you want to move to a window that has been completely obscured by another window, use the Task Manager (explained in the next section) to make the switch, or close or resize the foreground window to get access to the hidden window. Figure 3-2 shows a screen with several open windows.

You can close an open window in one of two ways: minimize it to an icon or quit the task. You can minimize a window to an icon also in two ways: press the down-arrow icon in the window's upper-right corner, or choose Minimize from the Control menu. You can quit a task by double-clicking on the Control menu icon in the upper-left corner or by choosing Close from the Control menu; application windows also usually have an Exit option on their File menu.

*Figure 3-2: Open windows.*

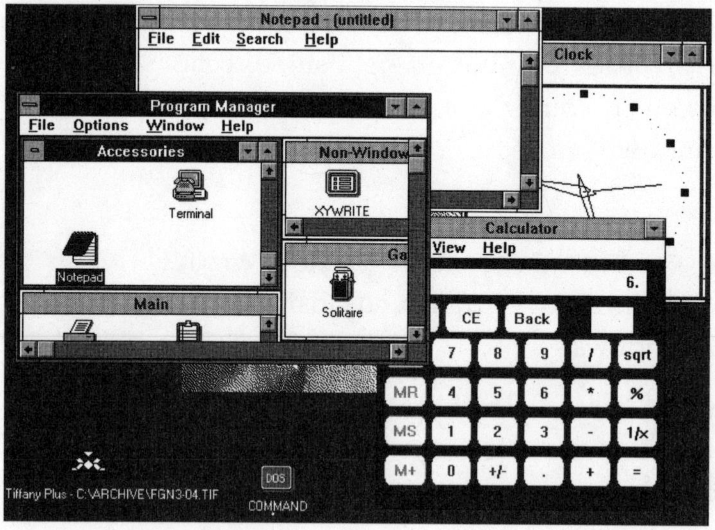

Minimizing a window gets it out of your way temporarily. But sometimes you want to see more of a window, not less. A full-size window lets you concentrate fully on the data it displays. The Maximize Control menu option, or the up-arrow icon in the upper-right corner of a window, will enlarge a window to full screen size. When you enlarge a window to full-screen size, the maximize icon changes to resemble a combination of the maximize and minimize icons. This icon can now be used to restore the window back to its original size. You can also restore the window to its earlier state using the Restore option from the Control menu; you will notice that many of the Control menu's other options are grayed out and therefore not available when a window occupies the entire screen.

You can change a window's size from any corner or side. Using a corner to resize a window will change its rectangular size, altering both its length and width. Resizing from one side (right, left, top, or bottom) changes just one dimension of the window's size. To resize a window with a mouse, move the screen pointer to a border and watch for it to change to a double-headed arrow. Then, press and hold the mouse button and move the mouse to resize the window. To resize a window using the keyboard, press Alt-Spacebar to display the Control menu and select the Size option. The pointer changes to a four-headed arrow icon. Use the arrow keys to resize the window; use the Esc key to cancel the operation.

Moving a window is often necessary to let you view two applications at once or to uncover a hidden window. To move a window without changing its size, place the screen pointer on the window's title bar, press and hold the mouse button, and move the mouse. To move a window with the keyboard, press Alt-Spacebar to display the Control menu. Then select the Move option. The pointer changes to a four-headed arrow icon. Use the arrow keys to move the window; use the Esc key to cancel the move.

One way to prevent a window from obscuring other windows is to turn on the Cascade or Tile options from the Program Manager's Windows menu. These options instruct Windows to place newly-opened windows in such a way as not to obscure other windows.

Cascading windows appear overlaid one upon the other while tiled windows appear side-by-side.

### *Switching Tasks*

An open window or an icon on the desktop represents a running task, and you will frequently need to switch from one task to another. You can switch tasks three ways: use the Task Manager, change active windows, or restore an icon to a window.

Pressing Crtl-Esc calls up the Windows Task Manager. You can also use any window's Control menu to select the Switch To option to bring up the Task Manager. The Task Manager (see Figure 3-3) displays a list of the currently running tasks with one task highlighted in reverse video. You can scroll through the list with the keyboard arrow keys or you can select a task by pointing at and clicking on its name. You can switch to the highlighted task by pressing the Switch To button (keyboard users press S while mouse users point and click).

*Figure 3-3: The Task Manager.*

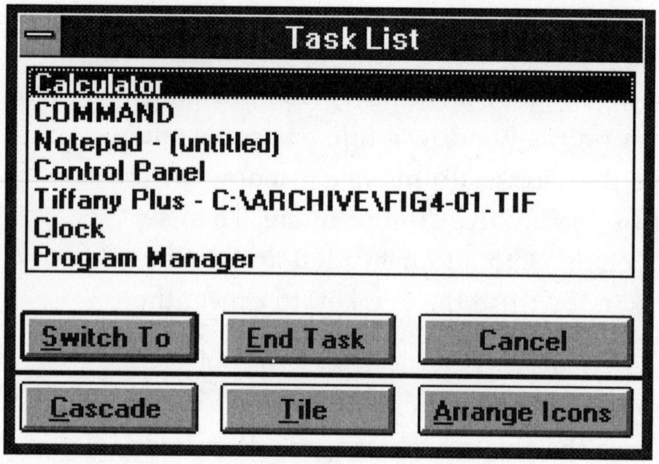


Task Manager also lets you end (quit) a task, cascade or tile the windows of the tasks on the screen, and arrange icons (align icons according to any currently active sizing grid).

### Menu Operations

Most of the actions that Windows can perform appear on a menu. As explained in the next chapter, every application usually has a menu bar with one or more menus. To get to the menu bar, press the F10 key or move the screen pointer to the menu area. Once there, press the keyboard arrow keys to move to a menu name and press Enter, or click the mouse button on a menu name to drop down that menu.

To make a menu choice, press Enter when a menu choice is highlighted in reverse video. You can change the highlighted option with the mouse or with the keyboard arrow keys. Keyboard users can also press the key that corresponds to an underlined letter in a menu option name to select that option.

Some menu options are on/off choices; selecting a choice places a check mark beside the name on the menu and activates that choice until you select it again to turn it off.

## Summary

Windows 3.0 runs in three different modes according to the hardware of the computer running it. Windows 3.0 can run applications written for earlier versions of Windows, but only under Real mode.

The essential skills for using Windows include using a mouse, interacting with windows and menus, and switching among tasks. With an understanding of these techniques, the next chapter takes you on a tour of the major components of Windows.

# CHAPTER 4

# *Getting Acquainted with Windows*

When you installed and then experimented with entering and leaving Windows, you experienced a few of its most notable features: the graphical screen with icons representing application programs and other tasks; the user-controlled way in which activities happen on the desktop; the increase in speed afforded by using a mouse to make selections; the use of pull-down menus for offering program selection choices which stay hidden until you need them; and a variety of message boxes, windows, and dialog boxes—little windows that pop-up to let you make some choice—for isolating different program options and actions.

This chapter explores the major components of Windows to familiarize you with its basic functions and appearance. The chapter also explores the Windows Help system.

## The Desktop

The visual command interface of an environment like Windows lets you use your eye to quickly spot a representation of a program or task instead of having to read a text label. Since over 50 percent of the human brain is devoted to processing visual images, seeing an icon rather than reading a program name is a natural way to interact with your computer.

You will make choices more quickly and find what you need with less effort.

Windows uses a desktop metaphor. A Windows screen is a graphical recreation of a typical desk. This desk has file drawers that you can open to reveal file folders that hold letters, spreadsheets, and reports. You will not find a stapler or a roll of Scotch tape on this desktop but you will see a clipboard, a Notepad, a paintbrush, and other tools that can let you work more efficiently with your computer.

Once you choose to use a tool on your desktop, that tool stays active until you put it away by closing it. This situation mimics the action of taking a tool out of a desk drawer and placing it on the desktop to be within easy reach. You can get an active tool out of the way on your desktop by shrinking it to an icon where it will appear in the icon area at the bottom of the screen. Every Windows tool opens a window on the screen when you make it active, and this open window has a minimize icon that you can click on to shrink that task to an icon. When you need that tool again, click on its icon to restore it to its open state.

Because interacting with Windows depends on making choices, either from menus or by pointing at icons, a mouse is an invaluable hardware tool. With a mouse, you can easily move windows and icons around on the screen, and you can adjust the size of a window so that you can see two or more windows on the screen at once. You can also perform these Windows operations with a keyboard, making heavy use of the arrow keys, with only a little more effort than using a mouse requires.

## A Windows Tour

Now let's take a close-up look at the Windows landscape. The main components of the Windows scene include windows, icons, and menus. The following description of these components will highlight the elements of Windows that you will use the most—the ones that make Windows a great productivity enhancer. We will take a closer look at how to use many of the less-often-used Windows components in Chapter 5.

### Anatomy of a Windows 3.0 Window

First, take a look at Figure 4-1 to view the anatomy of a window. This figure shows that a window has a *title bar*, a *Control menu icon* in its upper left-hand corner, *minimize* and *maximize icons* in the upper right-hand corner, *scrollbars* on the right side and bottom of the window, and a border around the outside of the whole structure.

A title bar shows the name of a program or task along with the filename of any file the program currently has open. The Control menu icon activates the pull-down menu (also called the *system* menu, described more fully in a later section) that lets you restore or close an application; move, resize, minimize, or maximize a window; or switch to the Task Manager without using the keyboard. The minimize and maximize icons let you shrink a task to an icon, or make a task full-screen. Scrollbars let you see the contents of an application or document display area that is not currently visible inside the window because it is larger than the window itself. Finally, the border shows you the boundaries of the window; the border disappears when you make a task full-screen. Table 4-1 summarizes the parts of a window.

*Table 4-1: A summary of the parts of a window.*

| *Control* | *Description* |
|---|---|
| title bar | The description at the top of a window that lists the name of the currently running application. |
| control menu icon | The icon that allows you to move or change the size of a window, or to quit an application. |
| minimize/maximize icons | These options can be clicked on to reduce an application to an icon and reactivate it later. |
| scrollbars | The vertical and horizontal bars that, when clicked on, show more information in a window or dialog box. |

*Figure 4-1: Anatomy of a Windows window.*

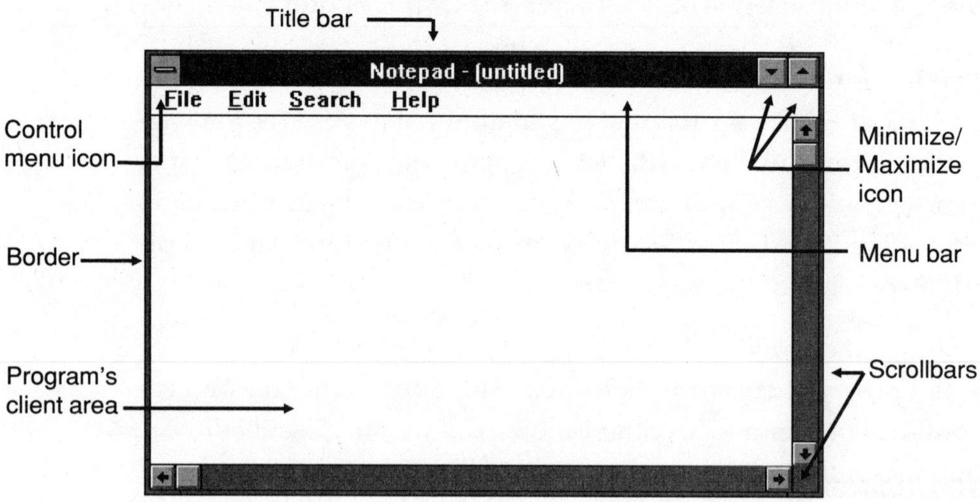


Though the difference is subtle, Windows uses two separate types of window: an *application* window, and a *document* window. Any running program, or task, inhabits an application window. The name of the application, along with the name and directory path of any file it is currently using, appears on the window's title bar.

A document window appears only with an application that can open more than one document at a time. A document window's appearance is similar to that of an application window's with the exception that a document window has no menu bar; it usually does have a Control menu.

Applications run inside windows most, but not all, of the time. Some applications, called non-Windows applications, occupy the entire screen when running and *do not* reside in their own window unless you run Windows in 386 Enhanced mode; Chapter 5 explores the differences between Windows and non-Windows applications in more detail.

Beside application and document windows, Windows uses smaller window-like boxes called *message* and *dialog* boxes. Message boxes simply display a message that you read and acknowledge by pressing Enter or clicking on an OK button inside the box. Usually, when a message box is on the screen, Windows will not respond to any input until you acknowledge the message. Dialog boxes provide a way to make a selection of some sort, such as choosing a program filename. Figure 4-2 shows a dialog box that appears when you select Run from the Program Manager File menu. This dialog box lets you type in a program name that Windows will then run just as if you typed that program name at the DOS prompt. Notice that a dialog box usually gives you the option to cancel the operation.

*Figure 4-2: The Run dialog box.*

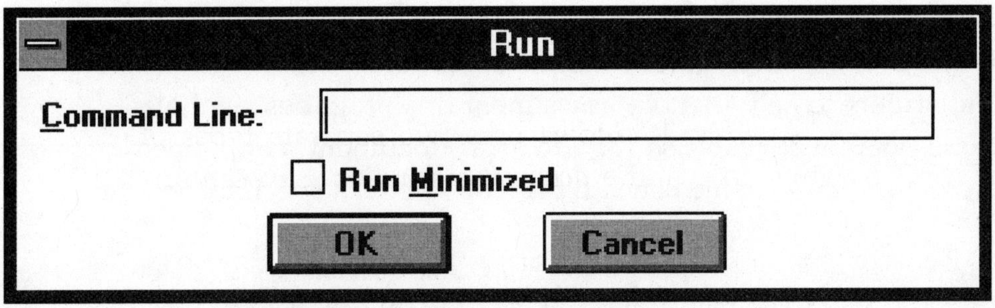


### *The Flexible Window*

Many of today's applications for PC-compatible computers use windows to isolate data on the screen. But a unique feature of environments like Windows 3.0 is their ability to change the size and the location on the screen of an application's windows. This window flexibility lets users arrange windows on their screens to suit any purpose.

Using a mouse or the keyboard, you can drag an open window to any location on your screen. Moving windows is useful if you want to see two or more open windows at once. You can also shrink a window in size from any side or corner. If you resize the window from its left side, for example, you make room on the left side of the screen where you can then move the resized window or open a second window.

Shrinking open windows to icons, as we have previously seen, lets you clear your desktop without shutting an application down. But you can also make an application's window full-size if you need to by using its Maximize button. Maximize and Minimize buttons always appear in the upper right-hand corner of a window when those functions are available. Maximizing a window to take up the entire screen makes documents easier to read and change.

### *Icons*

One of the major strengths of Windows is its use of pictorial symbols called icons. Icons visually represent a program, a task, or a document. Windows uses three different kinds of icon: application, program, and document icons. Different icons represent different kinds of objects to show the limits on how these objects can be used. Icons usually have a text label under them to help identify any similar or ambiguous symbols. Many separate documents can use the identical document icon, which requires you to refer to the name beneath the icon to pick a specific document.

Application icons represent a running application program. They only appear when you shrink a running program down to its icon. Application icons can appear on the Windows desktop outside the borders of any window. Applications icons can be moved around the desktop to any location. They cannot be moved inside a window.

Document icons appear when you minimize a document window inside an application window. The document icon stays within that application; it cannot be moved outside the application's window. Figure 4-3 shows a good example of document windows; inside the Program Manager window, notice the four document windows that contain groups of application and accessory programs. The contents of a document window depends on the application that owns the document. Frequently, document icons look identical to other document icons; only their labels distinguish them from one another.

*Figure 4-3: Program Manager's document windows.*

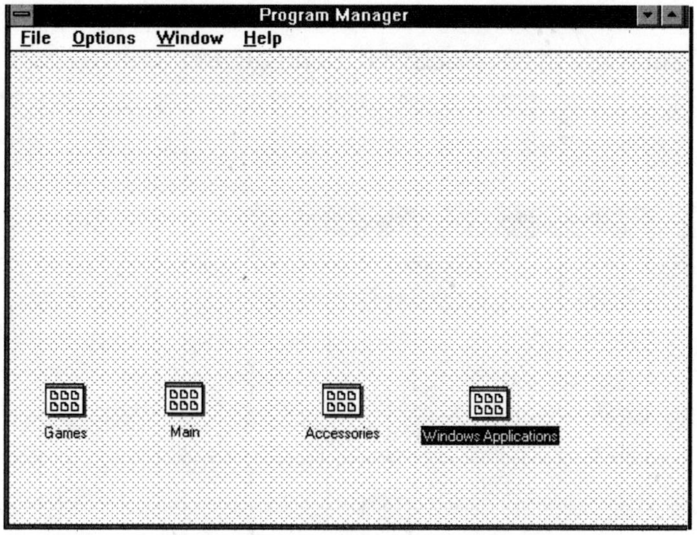


Program item icons identify utilities in the Program Manager document windows. These utilities include the DOS Prompt, File Manager, and other programs that are part of Windows itself. Figure 4-4 shows the program item icons in the Accessory group. Program item icons cannot be moved outside the Program Manager window, but they can be moved from one document window to another.

### Menus

An event-driven, point-and-shoot environment lives and dies by giving its user the ability to make choices. Menus make an ideal location for clustering choices of activities and selectors. As a result, Windows and its applications make heavy use of menus. Menu options stay hidden until you need them through the use of pull-down menus. Activating a menu, by clicking once on its name on the menu bar, causes it to drop down a list of menu options. Choosing an option from a menu causes that action to happen. You can also activate a menu by pressing the Alt or the F10 keys to activate a menu bar and highlight a menu name in reverse video.

Then, you can use the arrow keys to move the reverse-video highlight to the menu you want to activate where you just press Enter to make that menu appear. An underlined letter in a menu name lets you press Alt+ a single letter to activate a menu, such as Alt+F to activate a File menu.

*Figure 4-4: Accessory group icons.*

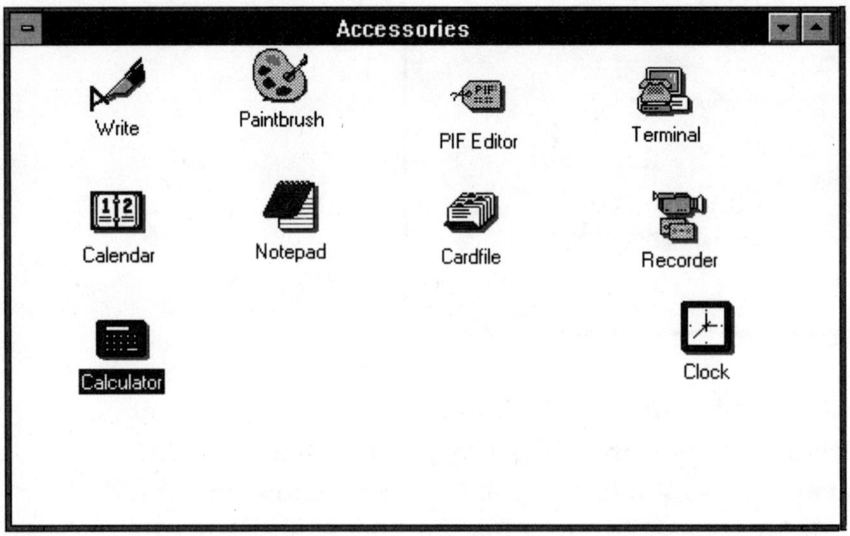


Figure 4-5 shows the Program Manager's activated File menu. As you can see, this menu offers many choices for performing file-related activities.

All application windows have a menu bar showing one or more menus. All windows, application or document, have a Control menu. You can make the Control menu appear by clicking its icon once with the mouse. Or, you can press Alt+Spacebar on the keyboard to drop down the Control menu (more on this menu in a later section).

Menus can also provide options that do not perform an action but instead act as a toggle switch to turn on or off some attribute or display criteria. For example, the File Manager's View menu lets you check off how you want to view files: by name, by type, or sorted in some way (see Figure 4-6). A check mark next to an option indicates that option has been chosen and it governs how file directories will be displayed.

*Figure 4-5: The Program Manager's File menu.*

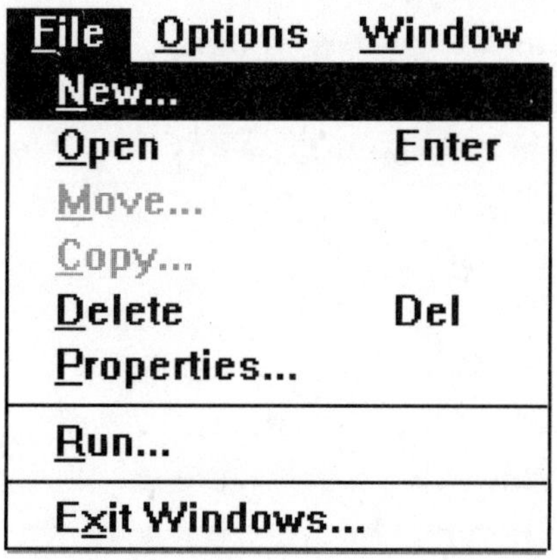


A look back at Figures 4-3 and 4-4 reveals some quirks about menus. Some options appear in light-gray text instead of black type, others have an ellipsis (...) after them, while still others have a keyboard key combination beside them. Each of these extra symbols has a distinct meaning.

*Figure 4-6: The File Manager's View menu.*

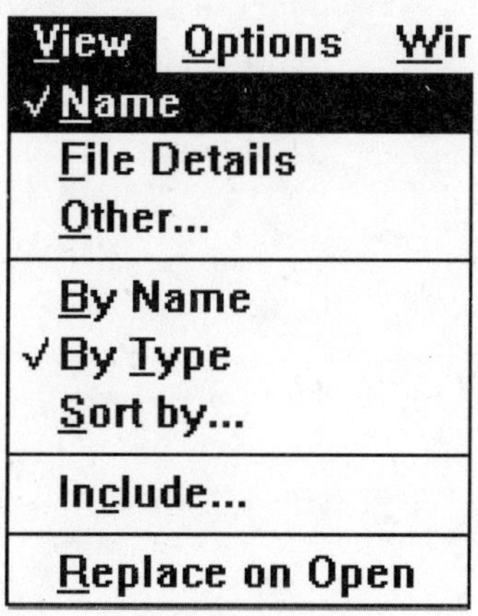

Light-gray text means an option is not currently available. You may have to make some other selection before the grayed out option can be used, or it just might not be available under the current circumstances. An ellipsis signifies that a dialog box will appear when that option gets chosen so that further information can be provided. A key combination after a command shows the keyboard shortcut, or *accelerator*, keys to use to activate that command or selection without opening the menu. An underlined letter in a menu option lets you choose that option by pressing the keyboard key for that letter. In Figure 4-5, for example, pressing D or the Del keys on the keyboard will activate the delete operation when the File menu is displayed.

### The Control Menu: A Specialty Menu

Every window has a special menu called the Control, or system, menu. This menu provides a way to restore an iconized window to its last state when open on the screen, or to close a window and thereby shut down a running task (pressing Alt-F4 is a keyboard shortcut for closing a task). The Control menu also provides a way to minimize or maximize a window; if you do not use a mouse, performing these functions would be awkward or impossible without the Control menu. Similarly, the Control menu has Size and Move options to permit changing a window's size or location without the aid of a mouse.

Table 4-2 shows some shortcuts for the Control menu's functions.

*Table 4-2: The Control menu's shortcuts.*

| *Command* | *Shortcut* |
|---|---|
| Restore | Alt+F5 |
| Move | Alt+F7 |
| Size | Alt+F8 |
| Minimize | Alt+F9 |
| Maximize | Alt+F10 |
| Close | Alt+F4 |

The Control menu is easily the Windows graphic that you will see most frequently since it opens on your screen for so many essential Windows operations. For example, a single mouse click on any active task's icon pops open the Control menu to let you close or restore that task.

### The Managers

Control over the computer environment is what Windows is all about. To provide this control, Windows provides several built-in accessory programs called *managers*. Windows uses three primary managers to control the computer's most important functions: running programs, managing disks and directories, and printing. These managers are named Program, File, and Print.

As you have already seen, the Program Manager plays a vital role in Windows. This manager controls access to all of Window's built-in accessories and utilities as well as access to application program groups that you create. We will explore the inner workings of creating such groups and other Program Manager functions in Chapter 8. For now, just remember that the Program Manager lets you run other programs as tasks.

The File Manager also plays an important role in Windows. Using this manager, you can perform all the many file operations crucial to the maintenance of a hard disk and its directories and files. Chapter 9 explores the File Manager in great detail and explains just how to do all the disk- and file-related DOS operations you currently perform on a daily basis from within Windows.

Conspicuously absent from Windows 3.0 is the DOS Executive that appeared in earlier versions of Windows. The DOS Executive has been replaced by the more robust File Manager in Windows. The Windows File Manager will be instantly recognizable to OS/2 users since it is virtually identical to the OS/2 Presentation Manager's File Manager.

The Print Manager provides an expanded print spooler feature to a DOS-based machine—a print spooler controllable by a user. All standard Windows applications create print files that get sent to the Print Manager. The Print Manager then controls the printing of that and any other files as a background task. This background printing lets you continue to work with your computer while printing takes place. You can send many files to the Print Manager without fear of losing print requests. Print Manager uses a special print queue to store print requests. You can inspect and modify the print queue at any time through the Print Manager. Chapter 7 explores the workings of the Print Manager in detail.

### The Clipboard

In a computing world where you can run more than one application at a time, the ability to move text or graphics from one program to another is not only nice, it is essential. Windows provides this capability using a facility called the Clipboard.

The Clipboard functions as a temporary storage area. You can put some text or graphic data on the Clipboard, switch to another application, and then copy the Clipboard's contents to the newly-active application. When you copy the Clipboard's contents into another application, the Clipboard retains the original information. You can then copy it again. The information on the Clipboard stays there until you clear the Clipboard. You could even place something on the Clipboard and leave it there until much later. As long as you do not put something else on the Clipboard or turn off your computer, any information you store there stays there.

For example, if you have some text on your screen that you would like to add to one or more other files, you could copy the target text onto the Clipboard, open another file, and paste the text into place. This operation is much less cumbersome than copying text into a temporary disk file and then merging that file with a second file.

Even more important than its procedural advantages, however, is the Clipboard's ability to move data between different applications. You would find it difficult if not impossible to take data from a Lotus 1-2-3 spreadsheet and copy it directly into a dBASE database. But the Clipboard can do just that for Windows applications. You can also move unformatted text to a non-Windows application. The Clipboard can even handle cut-and-paste operations with pictures or other graphic data for Windows applications.

What makes the Clipboard work, of course, is that all Windows application data exists as graphic information: even text is a graphic representation of letters and numbers. But Windows 3.0 can even perform cut-and-paste operations on non-Window applications. It will perform full-screen copy operations in Standard or Real mode, and partial-screen copies in 386 Enhanced mode. (A non-Windows program in Real/Standard mode can only capture full screens to the Clipboard.) The information copied to the Clipboard becomes a bitmap which can then be transferred to any program that can read bitmaps. You can paste unformatted text from a Windows application to a non-Windows program.

The Clipboard has its own menus that let you perform simple operations like saving the information on the Clipboard to a file, or deleting the Clipboard's contents. You can also load a Clipboard file from disk, view its contents, and copy that information into an application.

## The Windows Help System

A printed user's manual becomes almost superfluous with Windows. That is because much of the helpful information you need to use Windows can be placed right onto your screen any time you need this assistance. Not only does Windows provide on-line help for itself, it makes possible the addition of this kind of help to any Windows application. All the accessories that come with Windows provide on-line help, too.

You can tap into the Windows help system two ways. Any time you have a window open on your screen, you can press the F1 key to open a window that provides help on that task. Alternatively, selecting the Help menu from a window's menu bar displays the menu shown in Figure 4-7. Either way of calling for help brings up a Windows Help screen (see Figure 4-7). When you choose Help using a Help menu, you can then further choose to see a help index, information about using the keyboard instead of a mouse, assistance on basic Windows skills, and other topics. You can also highlight the name of a Windows utility, like the PIF editor for example, and press F1 to see help specifically for that utility.

*Figure 4-7: The Help menu.*

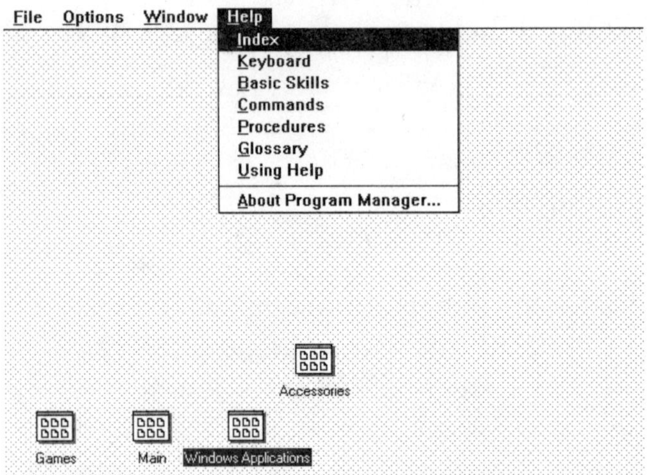


Once you have entered the help system, Windows provides several ways for you to navigate its volumes of on-line information. Windows help uses hypertext techniques that let you point to a word that appears in green letters, hold down the mouse button, and thereby display a text box that defines the word in question. There are also buttons at the top of the help screen just beneath the menu bar that you can push to bring up the index, or browse help topics in either direction.

One of the most useful features of the Windows help system is that it uses windows to display help; that means that you can size a help window to fit alongside an application window. That way, you can refer to help as you perform some operation you otherwise might find confusing.

*Figure 4-8: The Windows Help screen.*

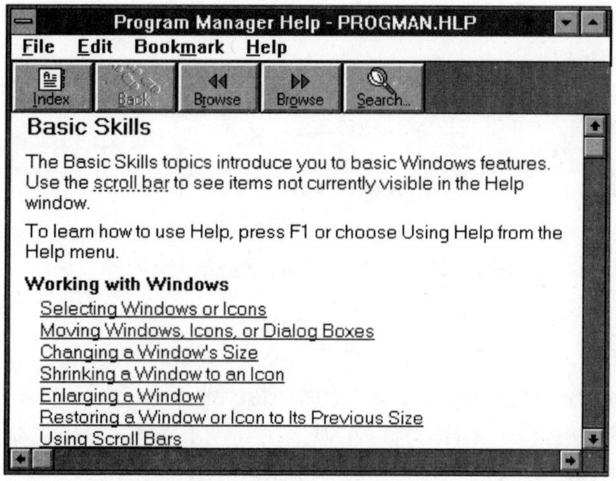


## Mouse or Keyboard?

By now, the advantages of using a mouse in a windowing, event-driven environment like Windows is probably clear. As you gain experience using Windows, however, you will likely discover that a combination of mouse moves and keyboard entries provides the best possible productivity.

For example, clicking on a menu is faster that pressing the Alt key to jump to the menu bar where you then have to choose a menu by using the arrow keys to move to the desired menu or by pressing the letter key that corresponds to the menu's first letter (F for file, H for help, and so on). Once you have chosen the menu, however, using a keyboard entry can sometimes be quicker that using the mouse. For example, most File menus use the Enter key to choose the Open option. Using that key can speed up your opening of files particularly if you use one hand to move the mouse and the other to press keyboard keys. So, clicking on an icon and then pressing Enter is the quickest way to open a document unless your hand-eye coordination for making mouse moves is top-notch.

Many people will be happy that they can use Windows without a mouse; not everyone feels comfortable using mechanical rodents. Windows keyboard access works surprisingly well, in contrast to the Apple Macintosh where using the keyboard becomes a real chore.

## Summary

As you have already seen, starting an application from Windows is a simple process. You simply double click the mouse on its icon, click once on the icon and press Enter, or move the blue highlight bar to the name under the application's icon using the keyboard arrow keys and press Enter. You can also select the Run option from the Program Manager's File menu and then type in the name of a program to run, just as you would at the DOS prompt. Once the application is running, you can switch to another application by calling up the Task Manager with the Crtl-Esc key combination and switch to any other running application.

Since all Windows operations take place within a running task, you never leave Windows when you run an application. Windows is always there for you if you need to use any of its functions or accessories. This ability to run multiple tasks gives you great power to get the maximum use from your computer.

Now you know the major features that Windows provides to make your interaction with your computer a less tedious undertaking. You now have Windows installed and you can load it, exit from Windows to DOS, and end your Windows session. You know what features Windows provides to allow you run programs, manage files, and print documents—all at the same time if you desire. You also have seen how Windows uses the keyboard, a mouse, and an on-screen desktop to streamline your use of a computer.

In the next chapter, we will learn how to use Windows many accessories.

## CHAPTER 5

# *Using Windows*

Using Windows on a day-to-day basis will quickly change the way you think about interacting with a computer. This change will evolve from the new tactics you will be using: pointing with a mouse, making choices from menus, adjusting the size and position of individual screen windows, and moving quickly from one running application to another.

This chapter explores the techniques you will use to take advantage of Windows and its applications by describing the major Windows applications: Write, Paintbrush, Terminal, Calculator, Cardfile, Calendar, Clock, Notepad, and Recorder, plus the lighter side of Windows, the games of Solitaire and Reversi. Understanding how each of these built-in accessories works will prepare you to deal with virtually any Windows application.

## The Basics

With the basic techniques you learned in Chapter 3, you can perform any allowable Windows operation. The following sections will give you an opportunity to sharpen these skills while showing you how to start using the built-in productivity tools that Windows provides.

### Windows Accessories

Windows comes with 10 surprisingly full-featured productivity tools called *desktop accessories*. These accessories include a calculator, a text editor, a paint program, a word processor, a telecommunications program, an appointment calendar, a calculator, a clock, a business card file, and a keystroke or mouse move recorder. Figure 5-1 shows the icons for these accessories in the Program Manager's Accessories applications group document window.

The sections that follow will get you started using these accessories and give you some insights into Windows techniques.

*Figure 5-1: The desktop accessories.*

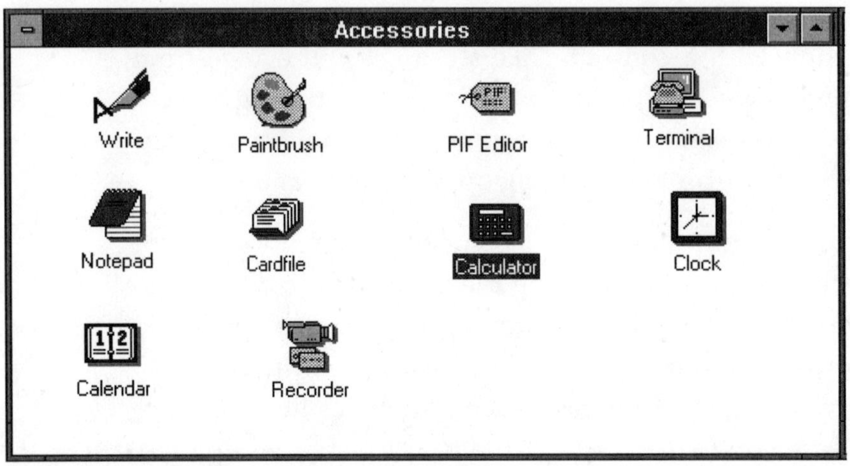


### Write

Write is a built-in word processor that provides the ability to display and print text in a variety of fonts and in a number of different point sizes. In addition to using mixed fonts, you can make individual letters, words, or blocks of text bold, italic, or underlined. Write allows super- and subscript characters, headers and footers, and will automatically number pages. Write lets you create hanging indents and will import graphics into a document. You can save a document with or without those embedded graphics.

The difference between Write and a more full-featured word processor like Microsoft Word is its relative slowness, lack of spelling checker and other utilities, and fewer formatting options. Nevertheless, for short documents like letters and memos, Write can serve many word processing requirements well. The description of Write that follows assumes you understand the basics of text editing and will get you started. Consult your Windows manual or the Write on-line Help text for a detailed description of Write's many features.

When you start up Write, the window shown in Figure 5-2 appears. Notice that this figure also shows the File menu dropped down to display its options, including New, Open, Save, Save As, Print, and so on.

*Figure 5-2: Write.*

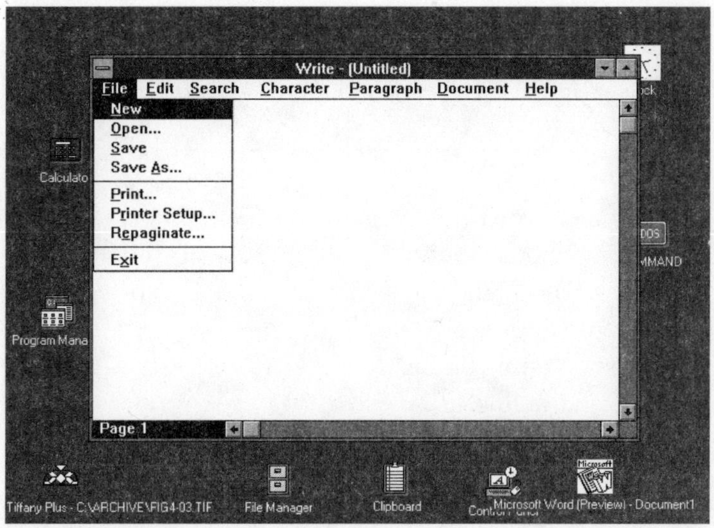


You can start a new document when you open Write by simply starting to type. A small star-like graphic symbol appears on the otherwise blank

Write screen; this graphic is the end-of-text mark. A flashing-line cursor shows you where the next character you type will be placed.

Once you have entered some text, you can begin to explore the many editing and formatting features of Write. You may want to start by saving what you have already entered. Choose the File menu's Save or Save As options to bring up a dialog box that prompts you to enter a filename. Save As is an option you would choose if you were editing a document that already existed on disk and you wanted to save the edited version under a different filename. If you chose Save instead of Save As, Write would replace the existing version of the document on disk.

Once you have entered a document that occupies more space than a single screen can display, you will want to be able to move around in the document. You can scroll with the mouse using the Write window's scrollbars, or you can scroll up and down through the document line-by-line with the keyboard arrow keys. In addition, you can use a variety of other key combinations to move around the text. Table 5-1 shows the available key combinations and their functions.

*Table 5-1: Keyboard combinations for navigating Write documents. (RIGHT and LEFT refer to arrow keys.)*

| *Keys* | *Function* |
|---|---|
| CTRL+RIGHT | Move to next word. |
| CTRL+LEFT | Move to previous word. |
| GOTO+RIGHT | Move to next sentence. |
| GOTO+LEFT | Move to previous sentence. |
| HOME | Move to beginning of line. |
| END | Move to end of line. |
| GOTO+DOWN | Move to next paragraph. |
| GOTO+UP | Move to previous paragraph. |
| CTRL+PAGE DOWN | Move to bottom of window. |
| CTRL+PAGE UP | Move to top of window. |
| GOTO+PAGE DOWN | Move to next page. |
| GOTO+PAGE UP | Move to previous page. |

| *Keys* | *Function* |
| --- | --- |
| CTRL+HOME | Move to beginning of document. |
| CTRL+END | Move to end of document. |

You can also use the mouse to place the screen pointer anywhere on the screen and press the mouse button to move the cursor to that location in the text.

The first Write feature experiment you will want to try is changing fonts. Before you can change fonts, make text bold or italic, or even edit text efficiently, you need to *select* the text. Selecting text is best done with a mouse. Place the screen pointer at the beginning of a section of text, press and hold the mouse button, and move the mouse. As you move the mouse, you will see that the text immediately behind the moving screen pointer is highlighted in reverse video. When you release the mouse button, this action stops. The highlighted text is now selected. To unselect the text, simply click the mouse button. To select all the text in a document, place the screen pointer at the left margin of the text, press and hold the Ctrl key and click the mouse button.

Once you have some text selected, you can change the font that text is displayed with (and will print with if your printer supports graphics). The Write default font is Courier. To change to another font, pull down the Character menu (see Figure 5-3). From this menu, choose the Fonts option to display the dialog box shown in Figure 5-4. You can scroll through the list of fonts in the small box and select one—Modern, for example. When you make this selection, the small box labeled Sizes shows a series of numbers from 6 to 48. These numbers represent point sizes for the chosen font. You can select any of these sizes or accept the default size (10). Press the OK button and watch Write change the text on screen to the Modern font. Rather than choosing the Fonts option, you could have selected one of the two fonts listed below Courier in the middle section of the Character menu. The Fonts option merely provides you with more font choices.

*Figure 5-3: The Character menu.*

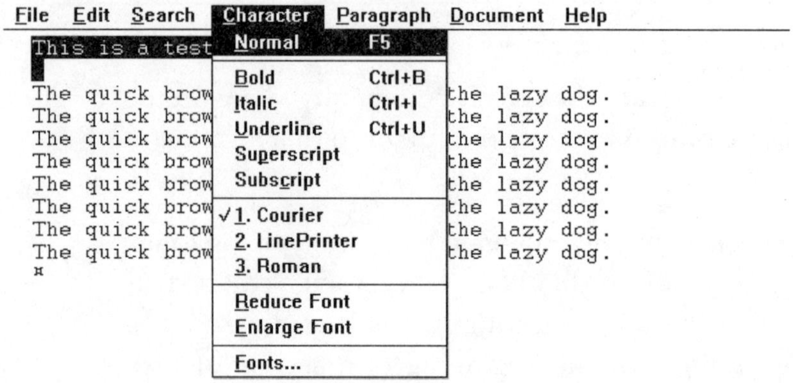


You can mark text and perform similar experiments with other options on the Character menu. You can make individual words bold or italic, for example, by first selecting the word and then choosing Bold or Italic from the Character menu.

*Figure 5-4: The Fonts option dialog box.*

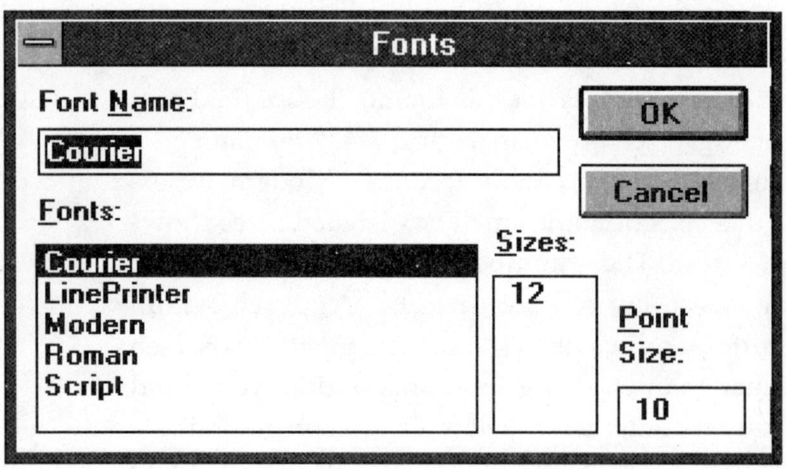

There are other operations you can perform on selected text. You can cut (delete) or copy selected text. When you cut text, that text stays on the Windows Clipboard until you remove it or place something else on the Clipboard; you can then paste it into another document, or into another spot in the same document it was cut from. Cutting and copying selected text uses the options on the Write Edit menu, shown in Figure 5-5. As you can see, this menu also lets you Undo the last change made to a document.

*Figure 5-5: The Write Edit menu.*

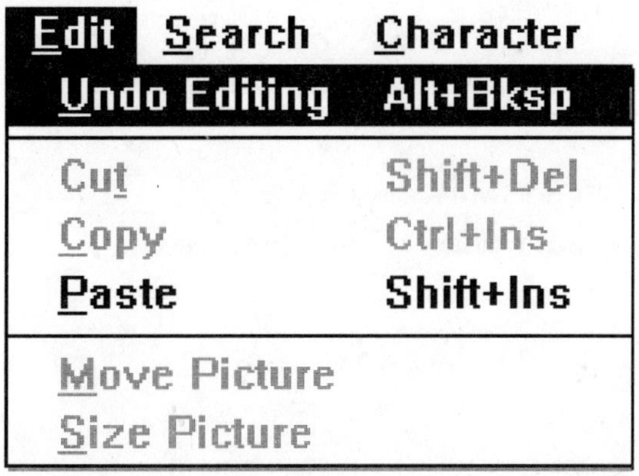


The Write Search menu lets you search a document for a word or phrase. A dialog box appears to let you enter the text to search for when you select Find from the Search menu. The Change option performs the classic search-and-replace operation.

The Paragraph menu offers options for aligning paragraphs on the left or right margins, or centering paragraphs between margins. It also provides an option to justify text between margins. This menu also provides paragraph line spacing options. These paragraph alignment and spacing operations can also be performed by choosing the Document menu's Ruler On option. This option places a ruler and some icons on the display just under the menu bar (see Figure 5-6). The icons are shortcut ways to specify paragraph alignment and spacing. You place the cursor anywhere in the paragraph you want to adjust and then click with the mouse on the appropriate icon to effect the change.

*Figure 5-6: The Ruler On option.*

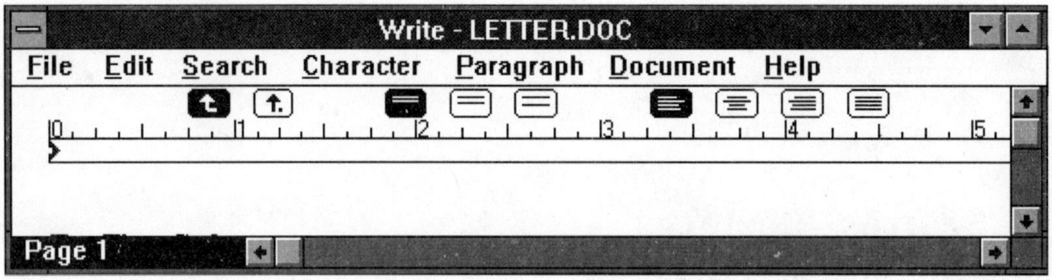


The Document menu lets you set up headers and footers for your document, and specify margins with the Page Layout option. This menu also lets you set tab stops for a document.

Write lets you save documents in Write format, Microsoft Word format (both of which preserve formatting and font choices), and as plain text. When you try to open a file that does not exist in one of these formats, Write lets you choose to covert the file to Write format or simply load the file as plain text.

### Paintbrush

Windows' Paintbrush accessory has been substantially upgraded from its earlier Windows version. Paintbrush lets you create simple or elaborate color drawings that can be merged into other applications. Paintbrush artwork can be saved as .PCX files, monochrome bitmaps, 16- or 256-color bitmaps, and 24-bit bitmaps.

The Paintbrush accessory's icon, a colorful artist's paint-mixing palette, resides in the Accessories group window of the Program Manager. When started up, Paintbrush displays the window shown in Figure 5-7.

Paintbrush's tools appear on the left side of the window and its color palette appears along the bottom. A small box that provides a variety of drawing line widths appears in the lower-left corner.

*Figure 5-7: The Paintbrush window.*

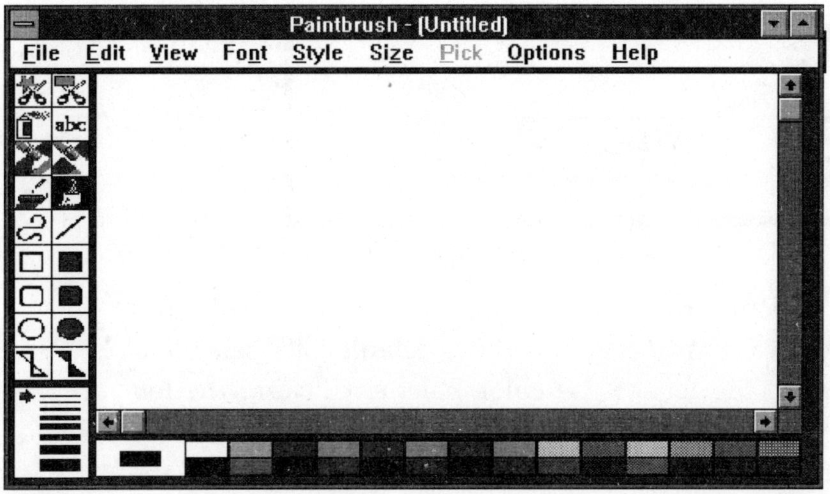


Paintbrush selects the Brush tool as the default upon startup. The Brush icon makes this tool look as if it might create wide brush strokes, but it actually produces strokes the width of the line selected in the line-width box, which defaults on startup to a thin, one-pixel wide line. You can change the shape of the Brush tool by double-clicking its icon with the mouse to display the dialog box shown in Figure 5-8.

You can immediately begin free-hand drawing in the white drawing area by pressing and holding the mouse button while moving the mouse. As soon as you release the mouse button, you stop drawing. If you do not like what you have just drawn, you can select Undo from the Edit menu to remove the last strokes you entered. To start over with a new drawing, select New from the file menu.

*Figure 5-8: The dialog box to change the Brush tool.*

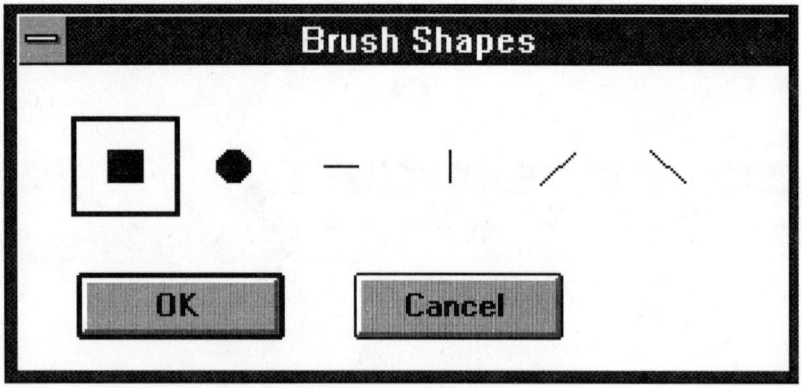


The default colors for Paintbrush drawings offer a white background and a black foreground color. You can view these default color selections in the small box just to the left of the color palette. Clicking the left mouse button on any of the colors in the palette changes the color of the small rectangle that indicates the foreground color. Clicking with the right mouse button changes the background color. For these color changes to take effect, you must choose New from the file menu after you have changed the color scheme.

The tools on the left side of the drawing window give you several options for creating artwork. There is a roller tool for filling in, or painting, an area; a tool for adding text; a spraying tool for creating shading effects; two kinds of erasers; two kinds of cutout, or selection, tools; and, a variety of tools for creating standard shapes like squares, rectangles, circles, and polygons. To use a tool, click on its icon with the mouse. The screen pointer usually changes shape to help you remember what tool is currently active.

The cutout tools, which appear at the top of the tools palette, let you select an area of a drawing for some other action like deleting or copying. The left cutout tool is a free-form tool that lets you choose any area regardless of shape. The right cutout tool selects square or rectangular areas on your drawing. Once you have selected an area from a drawing, the Edit menu's Cut, Copy, and Paste options plus the Pick menu's Flip Horizontal, Flip Vertical, Inverse, Shrink + Grow, and Tilt options become available.

The text tool lets you type text on your keyboard that becomes a part of your artwork. The Font, Style, and Size menus give you control over the typeface, type style, and point size of the text you add to a drawing.

The eraser tools let you completely erase an area, or you can change colors using the color eraser. The paint roller tool lets you fill in an area on the screen that is completely closed in by lines created with the brush, line, or shape drawing tools.

The line tool and the curved line tool let you add lines to a drawing. You create a line by placing the screen pointer where you want to start a line, pressing and holding the mouse button, and moving the mouse to the spot where you want to end the line. You can move the mouse virtually anywhere and the line stays between the begin point and the current location of the mouse. Curved lines also start out looking straight but once you have placed the line, you click with the mouse button on the side of the line where you want to see a curve to bend the line in that direction.

The tools for creating shapes work similar to the line tools. For squares and rectangles, press and hold the mouse button and move the mouse to see a box appear. As long as you hold the mouse button down, any mouse movement alters the size of the box. As soon as you release the mouse button, the box you have drawn is fixed in place. The circle tool works the same way. The polygon tool works a little differently. As you create sides to the shape you want, the tool stays active. Only when you close the shape by connecting two sides does the tool release. The shape drawing tools on the tools palette that are filled in with color produce boxes that immediately fill with the foreground color when you finish drawing them.

Once you have created some artwork, you can view the entire picture by using the View menu's View Picture option. This menu also has Zoom In and Zoom Out options that can provide you with other perspectives on your drawing. You can make the tool and color palettes invisible using other options from this menu.

The Options menu gives you a way to modify some of Paintbrush's default settings. For example, the Edit Colors option allows you to adjust the currently selected foreground color's red, green, and blue components. Figure 5-9 shows the dialog box that allows you to move a slider bar to adjust the proportion of the primary colors that make up the current foreground shade.

Any paint program like Paintbrush takes practice and patience to master. Fortunately, this experimentation process is often a great deal of fun.

*Figure 5-9: Adjusting the foreground shade in Paint.*

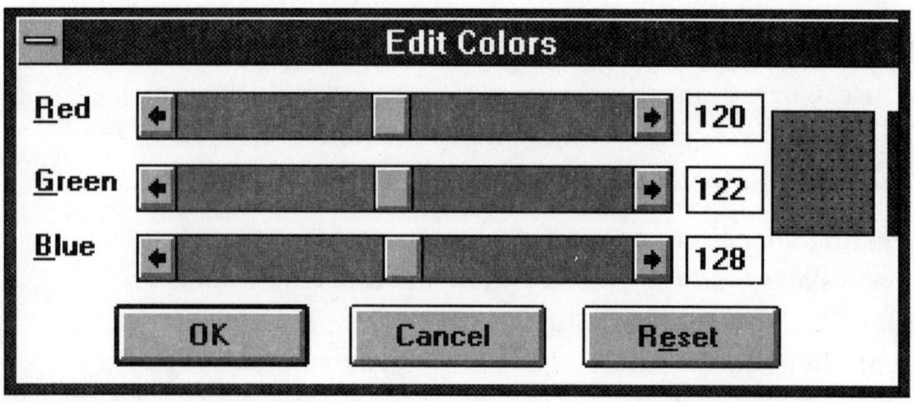


### Calculator

The Windows calculator accessory works just like a hand-held calculator that you might use to balance your checkbook or to perform a scientific calculation. The result of a calculation can be captured to the Clipboard for transfer to another application, and you can even paste data from another application into the Calculator's display window.

When you start up the calculator, the screen displays an accurate graphical representation of a real calculator, as shown in Figure 5-10. This screen-based calculator has number keys, operator keys, memory keys, and keys for special functions, such as square root and percentage calculations. You can press any of the number keys by clicking them with a mouse or by typing a number on your keyboard. You can press the special and operator keys by using mouse clicks or the keyboard key combinations shown in Table 5-2.

*Table 5-2: Keys for entering calculator functions.*

| *Keyboard Key* | *Calculator Key* | *Function* |
|---|---|---|
| + | + | Adds. |
| - | - | Subtracts. |
| * | * | Multiplies. |
| / | / | Divides. |
| @ | sqrt | Square root of the currently displayed number. |
| % | % | Percentage. 400*75% displays 300. |
| r | 1x | Reciprocal of the currently displayed number. |
| = or <ENTER> | = | Performs an operation on two numbers; pressing the key again repeats the operation. |
| F9 | +- | Changes the sign of the currently displayed number. |
| . or , | . | Inserts a decimal point. |
| Backspace or Left Arrow | Back | Deletes the last digit entered. |
| Delete | CE | Deletes the last number entered. |
| Esc | C | Deletes the last calculation entered. |
| Ctrl+C | MC | Deletes any value in memory. |
| Ctrl+R | MR | Displays any value in memory. |
| Ctrl+M | MS | Places the currently displayed value in memory. |
| Ctrl+P | M+ | Adds the value currently displayed to any value in memory. |

*Figure 5-10: The calculator.*

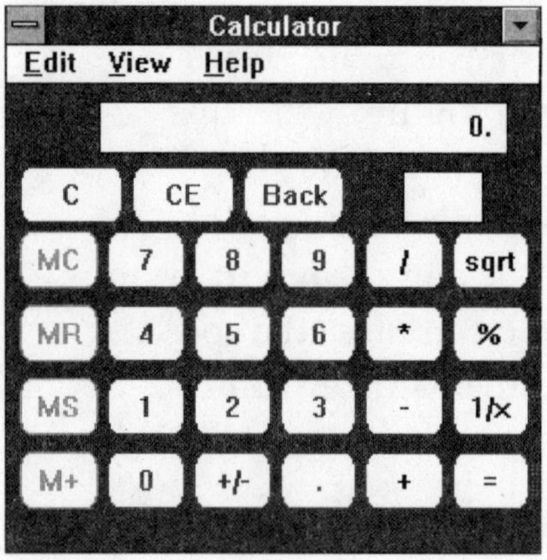


To add two numbers, for example, you would click the 1 and 2 keys to enter 12, then click the + key to signify add, and then click the 2 and 4 keys to enter 24. Next, press the = key or the keyboard Enter key, and the calculator shows 36 in its display window. Press = again and the display changes to 60, the result of adding 24 to the previously displayed 36. Press = again to see the result, 84.

The calculator has three menus, the last of which is the standard Windows Help menu. The Edit menu lets you copy the result of a calculation to the Clipboard or paste the Clipboard's current contents into the calculator display. The View menu lets you change the calculator into a more sophisticated scientific mode.

To copy a calculator result to the Clipboard, perform a calculation like the one described above. Choose the Copy option from the Edit menu and the number 84 gets transferred to the Clipboard. To verify that the transfer is complete, open the Clipboard to view it contents. Return to the calculator and press C to clear the display. Now choose the Edit menu's Paste option and 84 is reinserted into the calculator's display.

Pull down the View menu and choose the Scientific option. The calculator changes to look like Figure 5-11. This expanded calculator provides many additional functions, including a way to change a number from decimal to one of three other number systems—binary, octal, or hexadecimal. The functions that the scientific calculator provides are listed in Table 5-3.

*Table 5-3: The Scientific calculator's functions.*

*Operators*

<table>
<tr><th>Keyboard Key</th><th>Calculator Key</th><th>Function</th></tr>
<tr><td>(</td><td>(</td><td>Open parenthesis for grouping operands in a calculation.</td></tr>
<tr><td>)</td><td>)</td><td>Close parenthesis (see above).</td></tr>
<tr><td>&</td><td>AND</td><td>Calculates bitwise AND.</td></tr>
<tr><td>;</td><td>INT</td><td>Displays the integer portion of a calculated result.</td></tr>
<tr><td><</td><td>Lsh</td><td>Shifts left. Inv+Lsh shifts right. This operation is binary.</td></tr>
<tr><td>%</td><td>Mod</td><td>Displays the modulus, or remainder, of xy.</td></tr>
<tr><td>~ (Tilde)</td><td>Not</td><td>Calculates bitwise inverse.</td></tr>
<tr><td>|</td><td>Or</td><td>Calculates bitwise OR.</td></tr>
<tr><td></td><td>Xor</td><td>Calculates bitwise exclusive OR.</td></tr>
</table>

*Number Base Functions*

| *Keyboard Key* | *Calculator Key* | *Function* |
|---|---|---|
| F8 | Bin | Converts to the binary number system. |
| F4 | Byte | Displays the lower eight bits of the current number. |
| F6 | DEC | Converts to the decimal number system. |
| F2 | Dword | Displays the full 32-bit representation of the current number. |
| F5 | Hex | Converts to the hexadecimal number system. |
| F7 | Oct | Converts to the octal number system. |
| F3 | Word | Displays the lower 16 bits of the current number. |

*Advanced Statistical Functions*

| *Keyboard Key* | *Calculator Key* | *Function* |
|---|---|---|
| Ctrl+A | Ave | Calculates the mean of the values displayed in the Statistics Box. Inv+Ave calculates the mean of the squares. |
| Insert | Dat | Enters the displayed number in the Statistics Box. |
| Ctrl+D | s | Calculates the standard deviation with the population parameter as n-1. Inv+s calculates the standard deviation with the population parameter as *n*. |
| Ctrl+S | Sta | Activates the Statistics Box and the Ave, Sum, s, and Dat buttons. |
| Ctrl+T | Sum | Calculates the sum of values in the Statistics Box. Inv+Sum calculates the sum of the squares. |

*Other Advanced Functions*

| *Keyboard Key* | *Calculator Key* | *Function* |
|---|---|---|
| o | cos | Calculates the cosine of the displayed number. Inv+cos calculates the arc cosine. Hyp+cos calculates the hyperbolic cosine. Inv+hyp+cos calculates the arc hyperbolic cosine. |
| F2 | Deg | Sets trigonometric input for degrees. Use this function in decimal mode. |
| m | dms | Converts the displayed number to degree-minute-second format. Calculator assumes the displayed number is in degrees. Inv+dms converts the displayed number to degrees. Calculator assumes the displayed number is in degree-minute-second format. |
| x | Exp | Allows entry of scientific notation numbers. The exponent has an upper limit of +307. You can continue to enter numbers as long as you do not use keys other than 0-9. Exp can only be used with the decimal number system. |
| v | F-E | Toggles scientific notation on and off. Numbers bigger than 10^15 are always displayed exponentially. F-E can only be used with the decimal number system. |
| F4 | Grad | Sets trigonometric input for gradients when in decimal mode. |

| *Keyboard Key* | *Calculator Key* | *Function* |
|---|---|---|
| h | Hyp | Sets the hyperbolic function for sin, cos, and tan. The hyperbolic function automatically turns off after a calculation is completed. |
| i | Inv | Sets the inverse function for sin, cos, tan, PI, x^y, x^2, x^3, In, log, Ave, Sum, and s. The inverse function automatically turn off after a calculation is completed. |
| n | In | Calculates natural (base e) logarithm. Inv+In calculates e raised to the xth power, where x is the current number. |
| l | log | Calculates common (base 10) logarithm. Inv+log calculates 10 raised to the xth power. |
| ! | n! | Calculates factorial of the displayed number. |
| p | PI | Displays the value of PI (3.1415...). Inv+PI displays 2 * PI (6.28....) |
| F3 | Rad | Sets trigonometric input for radians when in decimal mode. |
| s | sin | Calculates the sine of the displayed number. Inv+sin calculates the arc sine. Hyp+sin calculates the hyperbolics sine. Inv+hyp+sin calculates the arc hyperbolic sine. |
| t | tan | Calculates the tangent of the displayed number. Inv+tan calculates the arc tangent. Hyp+tan calculates the hyperbolic tangent. Inv+hyp+tan calculates the arc hyperbolic tangent. |
| y | x^y | Computes x raised to the yth power. Inv+x^y calculates the yth root of x. |
| @ | x^2 | Squares the displayed number. Inv+x^2 calculates the square root. |
| # | x^3 | Cubes the displayed number. Inv+x^3 calculates the cube root. |

There is help text available for any of the functions that either the standard or the scientific calculator provides. The Help Index can direct you to the appropriate screen to obtain a description of any function. Since you cannot resize the calculator window when it is open, you may have trouble arranging the help window to view help text and the calculator simultaneously. You can use the mouse to bring either window into the foreground with one click; that will make switching back-and-forth as quick as possible.

*Figure 5-11: The Scientific calculator.*

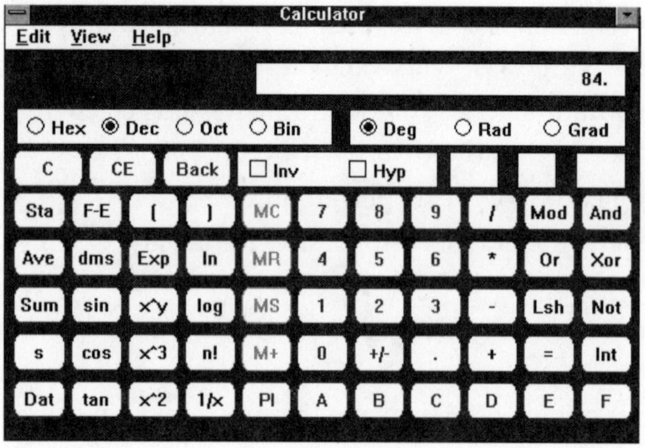


Calculator remembers the last mode it was used in; if you change from standard to scientific mode and do not change back, the calculator will open in scientific mode the next time you use it, even if you exit calculator and Windows.

### *Calendar*

The Windows Calendar accessory provides an electronic daily appointment book and a more traditional monthly calendar to help you keep track of important events. Calendar can track dates from January 1, 1980 to December 31, 2099. The Calendar accessory, denoted by a small desktop calendar icon, resides in the Program Manager's Accessories applications group.

Starting Calendar produces the screen display seen in Figure 5-12. The calendar window shows the current date and time in a *status line* area at the top of another display that lists the hours of the day in one-hour increments. A flashing cursor indicates where any text you type will appear. A line on the display below the last hour separates the *appointment area* from a *scratch pad* area. This is Calendar's daily appointment book mode.

*Figure 5-12: The Calendar.*

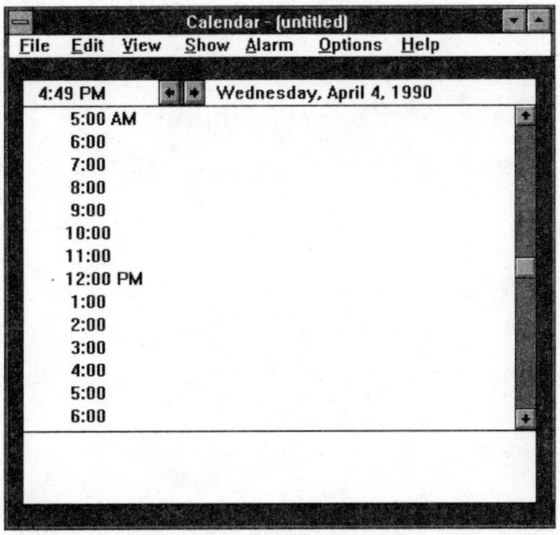


Pulling down the View menu offers an option to see a monthly version of the calendar. The keys F9 or M, as well as a mouse selection, can switch the display to a standard monthly calendar (see Figure 5-13). Once the monthly calendar appears on your screen, you can use the two arrow icons on the status line to scroll forward or backward through previous and future months and years. For example, if you needed to know what day of the week July 4th fell on, you could press the right-arrow icon until you reached July (my display started with April). If you double-click on the status line to the right of the arrow icons, you will return to the appointment book mode.

You can set Calendar to sound a warning beep on your computer to remind you of appointments. First, you should type in some text about the appointment next to the assigned hour. You can also add some explanatory text to the scratch pad area. Then, select the Set option from the Alarm menu. A small graphic bell will appear to the left of your appointment time. Selecting Set a second time turns the alarm off. When the appointed hour arrives, several things will happen. The computer's speaker will beep to alert you. If the Calendar accessory is open and active, a dialog box opens to remind you of your appointment. If the Calendar window is open but not currently active, its title bar flashes to signal the alarm. If the Calendar currently appears as an icon, the icon will flash to signal the alarm. Regardless of the Calendar's state, you have to acknowledge the alarm to turn it off by responding to a dialog box within the Calendar window.

*Figure 5-13: The standard monthly calendar.*

You can turn off the audible warning by selecting the Controls option from the Alarm menu. The check box labeled Sound, which is checked by default, can be unchecked to turn the alarm beep off. You can also use this dialog to instruct Calendar to sound the alarm up to 10 minutes early to give you some time to prepare for your appointment.

You can customize the appointment book to use 15 or 30 minute time increments instead of 60, and show a starting time other than 7:00 a.m. You can also set the calendar to display time according to a 24-hour, rather than 12-hour, clock. You can set a special time, a time that falls between increments on the appointment book, using the Options menu. The Options menu also provides a Mark option that allows you to mark a day with a symbol; you could mark all paydays, for example, to help you plan shopping expeditions.

Once you have created a calendar, you should save that calendar file so that closing the calendar accessory does not destroy your appointment schedule. Every week or so, you can use the Edit menu's Remove option to delete old entries and make room for new ones.

### *Cardfile*

The Windows Cardfile accessory simulates a set of index cards (see Figure 5-14). The cards can keep track of any kind of information—names, addresses, phone numbers, recipes, or dozens of other items. Any card file you create can be stored on disk, and the file sorts itself as you add cards to it so that the cards always appear in alphabetical order according to the index line on each card.

The index line is marked by the double line that appears just a short distance down from the top of a card. Underneath the index line is the area where you record information about an entry. This area accepts text and graphics. The area above the index line holds the descriptive text—a last name, for example—that Cardfile uses to sort the cards in the current file.

You can enter or edit the text for the index line for the card in the foreground by using the Index option on the Edit menu. When you add a new card to the file with the Add option from the Card menu, a dialog box opens to let you enter index-line information for this new card.

Once you have several cards in a file, moving from one to another is easy. The right and left arrow icons just below the menu bar let you browse forward and backward through cards. You can also move among cards using the keyboard key combinations shown in Table 5-4. The Search menu lets you Go To a specific card, while Find lets you locate a specific piece of text on a card.

*Figure 5-14: The Cardfile.*

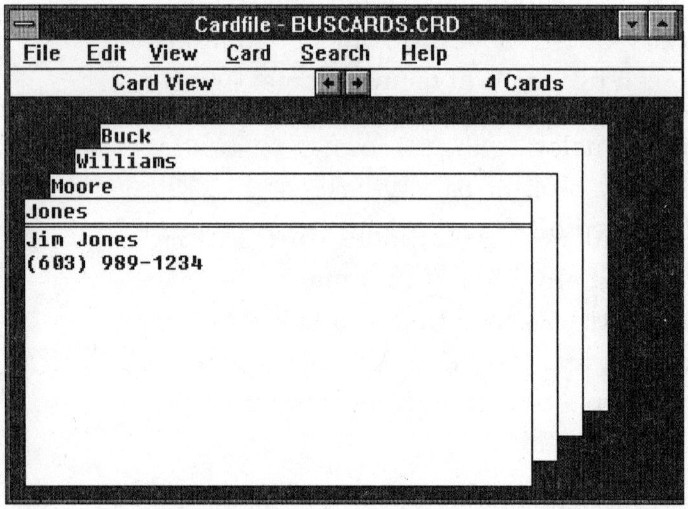


*Table 5-4: The keys for navigating Cardfile cards.*

| *Key(s)* | *Function* |
|---|---|
| PgDn | Scrolls forward one card. |
| PgUp | Scrolls backward one card. |
| Ctrl+Home | Brings the first card in the file to the front. |
| Ctrl+End | Brings the last card in the file to the front. |
| Ctrl+letter | Brings a card to the front of the file. Cardfile displays the first card whose index line begins with the letter. |
| Ctrl+Esc | Opens the Task List dialog box. |

When you have a large number of cards in a file, viewing the cards themselves is not the most efficient way to display the file. The View menu lets you choose to look at your file as a list of index line phrases. You can scroll through this alphabetical list to quickly move to a specific card, even if you do not remember the exact spelling of its index phrase.

Cardfile lets you merge two files, and it can print a single card or an entire file. You can also use Cardfile to initiate a telephone call on your modem by automatically dialing a phone number from a card using the Autodial option from the Card menu.

### Clock

The Windows Clock accessory is simply a visible way for your computer to display the time of day in either analog or digital format. Computers with an 80286/386 processor have a built-in battery-backed clock that runs even when the computer is turned off. The Clock accessory uses the information generated by this system clock to provide the display shown in Figure 5-15. The only user-controllable option for Clock is a Settings menu choice of Analog or Digital.

*Figure 5-15: The Clock in analog mode.*

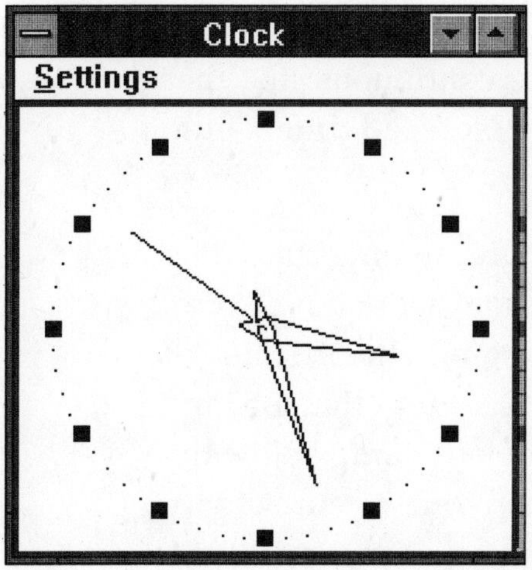

### Notepad

The Windows Notepad accessory is a text editor for keeping track of notes and memos. It has very few formatting options and uses only the system default font for displaying or printing text. Figure 5-16 shows an active Notepad window.

*Figure 5-16: The Notepad.*

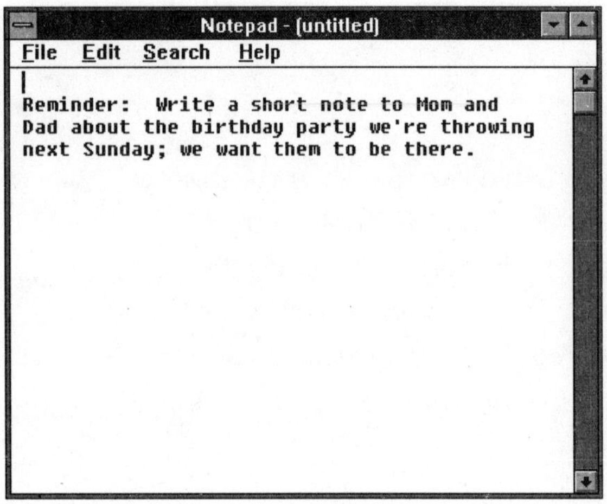


The first thing you should do when you start a Notepad session is to pull down the Edit menu and select the Word Wrap option. This choice will prevent the text you type from appearing as one continuous line that scrolls from right to left. From that point on, using Notepad differs little from using any other text editor.

Notepad provides one unusual and useful feature: a time and date stamp that you can use to create a personal log of your work day. To create a log, type the characters, ".LOG" at the left margin of the first line of a new file. Save the file under any name you choose. From then on, any time you open that file, Notepad places a time and date stamp below the last line of the file. You can then type notes about your recent activity and store the file. When you want to add more notes, open the file and append text after the most recent date/time stamp.

The Edit menu also offers an option labeled TimeDate. You can select this option (or press F5, the TimeDate shortcut key) to add the current date and time to any text you are creating. This addition might prove useful if you use Notepad to take occasional notes during a telephone call or meeting in your office, rather than keeping a running log.

You select text within Notepad in the same way as in Write except that Notepad has an Edit menu option for selecting all the text in a file. All you can do with selected text in Notepad is Cut or Copy it.

The maximum size for a Notepad file is 50,000 characters. To find out how close you may be to reaching this limit, choose the Help menu's About Notepad option to view a message box that shows the number of characters in the current file at the bottom of the box.

### *Recorder*

The Windows Recorder accessory lets you record keystrokes or mouse moves and save those sequences in a file. These sequences, called *macros*, can then be played back by Recorder to reproduce the recorded actions. Using macros is useful for repeating often-used operations. For example, if you open the Calendar accessory every Monday and set an alarm for a Tuesday lunch date with your boss, you could record the operation with Recorder and then execute it on Monday mornings with its shortcut key.

Macros of keystrokes work better than macros that contain mouse movements because mouse moves recorded in one window often do not work well when played back in a window of a different size. The default recording mode of Recorder saves all keystrokes and mouse click and drags, that is, when a mouse button is pressed. You can change this recording mode to ignore the mouse and record just keystrokes, or to record everything, including all mouse activity regardless of mouse button clicks.

When you choose the Record option from the Macros menu, a Record dialog box like the one in Figure 5-17 opens to display all the other options you can set for macro recording. In this dialog box, there are smaller labeled boxes for defining the shortcut key you will later use to play back your macro, defining the scope of your macro relative to a window or the entire screen, controlling playback speed, and setting the level of mouse activity you want to capture. The default settings for these options will be suitable for most macros.

*Figure 5-17: The Record Macro dialog box.*

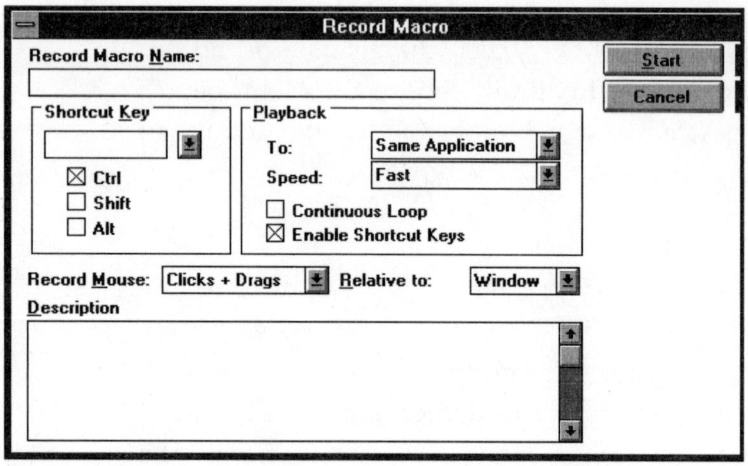


Once you have recorded a macro, you play back or execute the macro by using its shortcut keys when defined. If no shortcut keys were defined, you play back a macro with the Run option from the Recorder's Macro menu. Since you must choose a macro for playback before you can start it, the Recorder accessory window must be open in order to play back any macro. Once you start the macro, Recorder shrinks to an icon.

Recorder allows you to nest macros within a macro up to five levels deep. You must turn shortcut keys off to nest macros, and a higher macro calls a nested one by name. Many separate macros can occupy a single macro file but only one macro file can be open at any time. Recorder works only with Windows applications.

One use of Recorder is to create demos of programs or operations. Macros can be set up to play back quickly or at the speed they were recorded. For a demo, playing back a macro at the speed it was recorded gives the best results. A check box in the Record dialog box allows setting a macro to repeat continuously, which is helpful for macros used for a demo.

### *Terminal*

The Windows accessory called Terminal is a telecommunications application that lets your computer exchange information with another computer. The link between computers can be direct, via a cable, or over telephone lines using an intermediary device called a modem. The description of Terminal that follows assumes you understand the basics of computer communications.

The Terminal accessory's icon is a small computer with a telephone sitting on the keyboard; you will find the icon in the Accessories applications group window of the Program Manager. When you start Terminal, the window shown in Figure 5-18 appears. At this point, Terminal is in a terminal emulation mode with the ANSI-standard DEC VT-100 emulation set as the default.

From this point, you can perform a variety of alterations to the default settings for Terminal. The fastest way to make such changes is to load a *settings file.* A settings file is simply a file created by making changes to Terminal's default settings and then saving those changes to a file; Terminal appends a .TRM extension to a settings file when you choose the Save or Save As options from the File menu and assign it a name.

The first settings you will want to adjust will be those used by the computer to which you plan to communicate. These settings, which appear in a dialog box when you choose Communications from the Settings menu, include Baud Rate, Data bits, Parity, Flow Control, and Connector and also include check boxes to toggle on Parity Check and Carrier Detect. Click on any of the buttons beside a value for one of these settable options to choose that value.

*Figure 5-18: The Terminal accessory.*

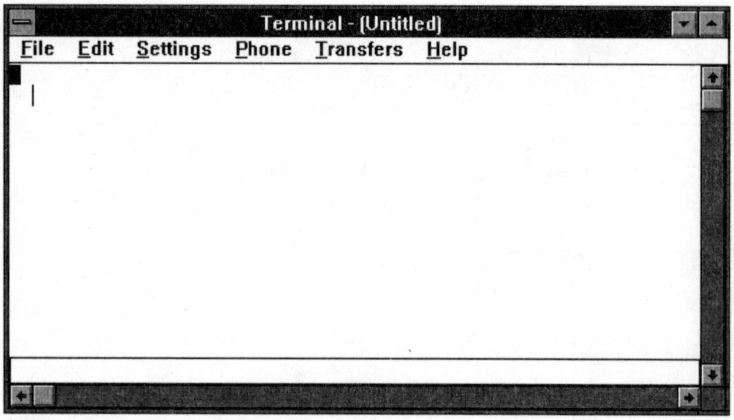


With no further adjustments, you could now choose the Phone Number option from the Communications menu and enter a number. Then, selecting the Dial option from the Phone menu will direct your Hayes-compatible modem to dial the given number. You will shortly be on-line to another computer.

Once on-line to another computer—a conferencing service like BIX or Compuserve for example—you can read messages and e-mail, and upload or download messages and files. The Transfers menu offers several options for sending and receiving both text and binary files. The only transfer protocols that Terminal offers for binary file transfers are XModem and Kermit.

Should you discover once you are on-line that the other computer uses a 132-column screen, for example, you can use the Settings menu's Terminal Preferences option to display the dialog box shown in Figure 5-19.

This dialog lets you choose options such as how you want the cursor to look, and what column width you want Terminal to use.

*Figure 5-19: The Terminal Preference option.*

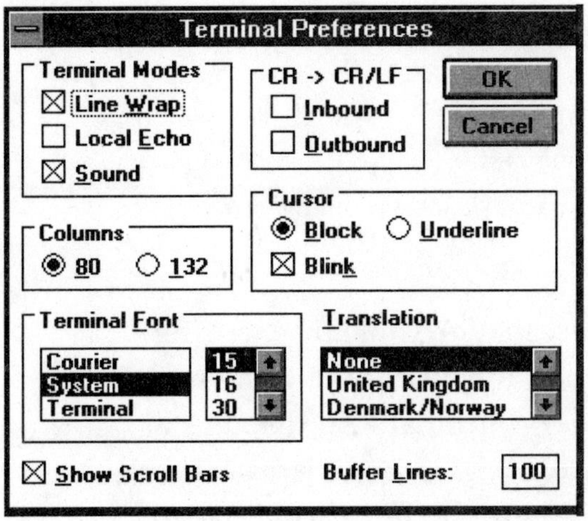


You can assign frequently-typed phrases to your computer's function keys that you can then press to send that phrase to the remote computer. For example, to reach the e-mail subsystem on BIX, you must type "mail" at the BIX prompt. Assigning the phrase "mail" to a function key lets you enter that phrase with a simple key press. A quirk of Terminal is that even though you can assign phrases to the F1-F9 functions keys, you must press and hold Ctrl+Alt and then a function key to actually issue the command phrase. The function-key assignment subsystem also has a primitive script language that allows you to build sign-on scripts. The script codes and their functions appear in Table 5-7.

*Table 5-7: Terminal's script control codes and their functions.*

| *Control Code* | *Function* |
|---|---|
| ^A to ^Z | Sends control code A to Z to the remote computer. |
| ^$D<NN | Causes Terminal to delay the specified number of seconds before continuing. |
| ^$B | Causes Terminal to transmit a break code of 117 milliseconds in duration. |
| ^$C | Chooses Dial from the Phone menu. |
| ^$H | Chooses Hangup from the Phone menu. |
| ^$L1 to ^$L4 | Changes to another level of key groups in which keys are defined. |

When the function keys you have assigned are made visible by choosing the Settings menu Show Function Keys option (or by checking the box Keys Visible in the Function Keys dialog box), Terminal also displays a small digital clock in the lower-right corner of the window display. The Settings menu provides an option called Timer Mode to turn this clock into a timer that will monitor your on-line connect time. Using this Timer Mode can help you avoid running up exorbitant on-line charges.

When you have signed off the remote computer and finished an on-line session, choose Hangup from the Phone menu to disconnect your modem from any open phone line. Then, you can exit Terminal. A dialog box will appear upon choosing to exit to give you a chance to save the current settings to a file.

### Games

Every computerist needs a distraction from everyday tasks on occasion. Windows gives you two desktop accessory programs that let you take a break from real work when you need to. Solitaire and Reversi will let you have some fun during your workday.

Solitaire really shows off the graphics capability of computers with EGA or VGA displays. Figure 5-20 does not do justice to the look of Solitaire since it does not reproduce the color of the actual display.

Solitaire can be played with standard or Las Vegas scoring rules. You can set the game up to play with a Draw One or Draw Three option for turning over cards in the deck. There are 10 different graphic designs for the back of cards and you can change them at will using the Game menu's Deck option. Some of these designs even feature animation; watch the sun carefully when you use the "beach" card motif.

*Figure 5-20: Solitaire.*

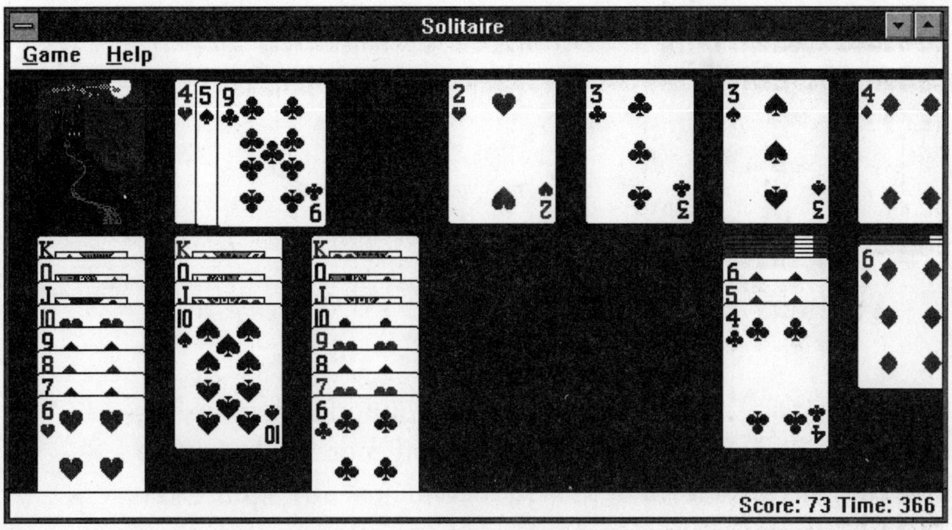


You move cards from one location to another by dragging them with a mouse. If you attempt to move a card where it is not allowed, it will simply be moved back to its original location; you cannot cheat with this version of Solitaire! But the good news is that you can win occasionally and when you do, you will be treated to an exciting animated display of cascading cards.

Reversi is a computer version of a board game called Othello (see Figure 5-21). The object of Reversi is to end the game with more of your game pieces (circles) on the board than your opponent. Unfortunately, your opponent is always the computer who plays a very good game even in the Beginner mode, which is one of four modes you can select.

*Figure 5-21: Me losing at Reversi.*

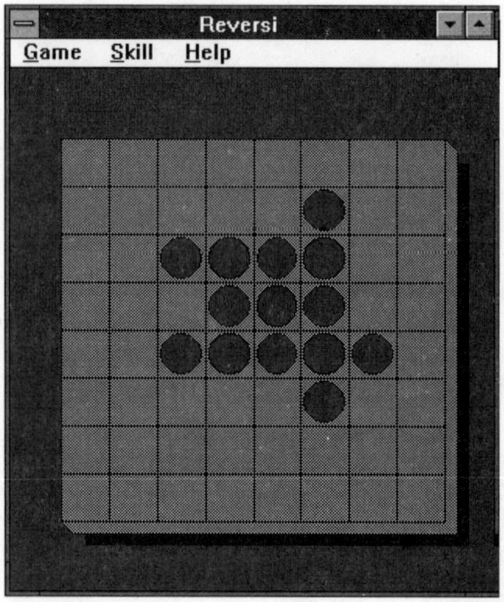


In Reversi, when you place a game piece next to an opponent's piece, his piece becomes yours along with any other adjacent pieces that form a row, column, or diagonal. You cannot place a piece in just any square; the only squares you can move to are squares adjacent to an opponent's that trap one or more of his game pieces between your own. When you make the move, his circle pieces change color and become yours.

Legal moves change the screen pointer to a cross as you move the mouse around the game board. As long as the pointer remains an arrowhead, a move to the square under the pointer is illegal. Figure 5-21 shows the early stages of a game in which the computer (dark circles) has a lead over a hapless human opponent (me).

## Summary

Mastering a few basic techniques regarding mouse usage, window management, task switching, and using menus lets you tap into the power of Windows. The accessories Windows provides can aid your productivity in a variety of ways. From word processing using multiple fonts to creating custom color bitmap images, Window's accessories give you many ways to get the most of your computer. Game accessories even realize the novel idea of letting you have fun with your computer.

Chapter 6 will further your education about specific Windows features and customizing it for your tastes.

## CHAPTER 6

# *Inside Windows*

One of the best things about DOS is its flexibility. You can use DOS to set up your machine in a variety of configurations. DOS has a way to load special drivers for adapting new hardware to the computer and for setting up the computer to use the hardware in a certain way. DOS has a batch control language that lets you write small programs to perform often-repeated operations. You can use these resulting batch (.BAT) files to automatically load applications and to streamline the operation of your computer.

Windows does not interfere with the ability you have to streamline your computer using DOS batch files. Many of Windows' features, like its built-in editing tools, can even make setting up and using special control files (like batch files) easier. Windows also provides ways to let you interactively change hardware settings in a much easier way than DOS. And, Windows has many built-in functions to let you modify and customize Windows itself for your computer.

This chapter shows how you can control the look and feel of Windows. This discussion explains how to use the Windows customization tools like the Control Panel and Setup. This chapter assumes that you now have Windows running on your computer and that you understand how to get around within its environment. Before looking at how to alter the look of Windows, let's define some of the special meanings of the words used in this chapter to describe Windows.

## Windows Terminology

Some of the words in the Windows lexicon have already been introduced—terms like "double-click" which describes the action of pressing twice in quick succession on a mouse button. Table 6-1 lists some other Windows terms you will need to know.

*Table 6-1: Windows terminology.*

| *Term* | *Description* |
|---|---|
| active | An area, application, or icon that will be affected by the next operation, such as a keystroke, mouse action, or command. Active windows have a colored title bar while inactive windows have a grayed-out title bar. |
| cascade | A way of arranging windows so that no window's title bar is ever covered by another window. This allows you to make a partially hidden and inactive window active—and visible—by clicking its title bar with a mouse. |
| check box | A small rectangle you can click on to turn on a selection. That selection stays active until you click on the box a second time, which turns the selection off. |
| choose | To make a window, icon, or application active. |
| click, double-click | A single or double press of a mouse button. |
| client area | The portion of a window where application data is displayed. |
| desktop | The area on the screen that Windows uses to display icons and windows. |
| direction keys | The keyboard arrow keys. |
| document icon | An icon that represents a document. |

| *Term* | *Description* |
|---|---|
| drag | To select and move a window or icon by holding down a mouse button while moving the mouse. This action moves the screen object under the mouse pointer in the direction the mouse is moved. |
| group | A related assemblage of documents or applications. |
| icon | A graphical symbol, frequently a small picture, that represents an application or document. |
| option | A dialog-box choice. Check box options are non-exclusive choices while option buttons are mutually exclusive. |
| point | To indicate an item for selection by moving a pointer around the surface of the screen. |
| program item icon | The picture that appears in a group window and represents an application you can start up. |
| select | The act of specifying an item without causing an action to take place. |
| wallpaper | A backdrop for the Windows desktop. |

If you run into any other words you do not understand, refer to the Windows glossary in an appendix of your Windows' user manual. Alternatively, select the Program Manager's Help menu, choose the Glossary option, and search for the word you need more information about. Figure 6-1 shows a window displaying a portion of the Windows' Help Glossary.

## Controlling the Look and Feel of Windows

Windows controls the look and feel of any computer on which it is installed, but you will be relieved to learn that you have a substantial amount of control over how Windows itself looks and reacts. This control is provided by two built-in Windows applications: the Control Panel and Windows Setup (we discuss setup in Chapter 7).

*Figure 6-1: The Help Glossary.*

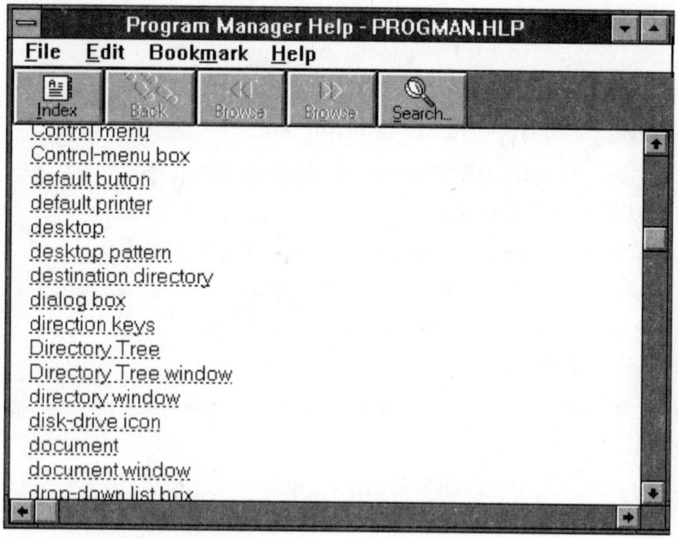


### The Control Panel

The Control Panel icon resides in the Main application group of the Program Manager and its icon looks like a miniature computer with a clock and a mouse attached (see Figure 6-2). The Control Panel is the primary way for you to make adjustments to the appearance and operation of Windows.

To activate the Control Panel, double-click the mouse on its icon or move the blue highlight bar to the label beneath the icon using the keyboard arrow keys and press Enter. This action opens the Control Panel document window shown in Figure 6-3. There are 10, 11, or 12 icons inside this window depending upon whether your machine is hooked to a local area network (LAN), or uses an 80386 processor chip. Each of the icons represents a dialog box that you can open to change or to set some aspect of the Windows environment.

*Figure 6-2: The Program Manager with the Control Panel selected.*

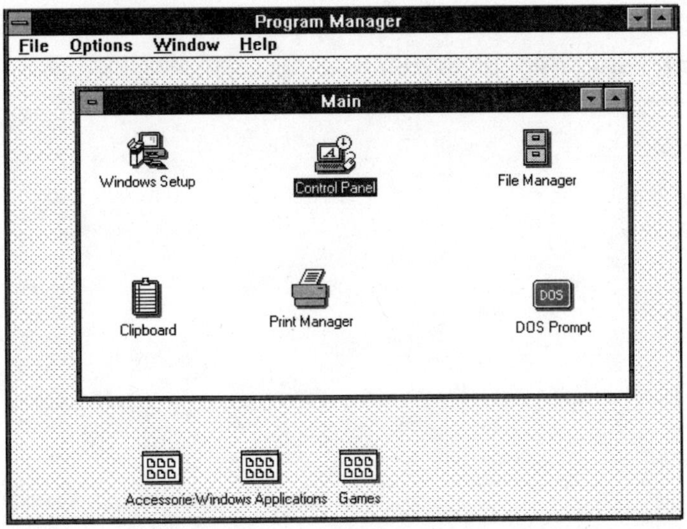


*Figure 6-3: The Control Panel document Window.*

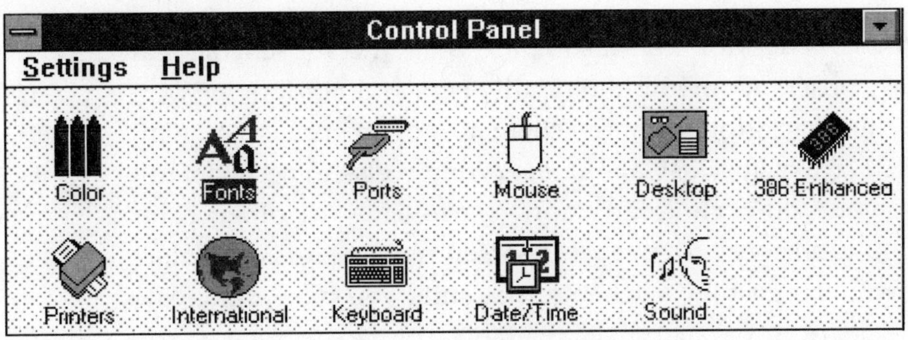


There are two ways to activate one of these dialogs. The first is to double-click with the mouse button or use the keyboard to launch the selected dialog. The second method is to click on the Settings menu to drop-down the menu shown in Figure 6-4. Each of these menu options can in turn be selected with a mouse click or a keyboard operation, such as using the down arrow key to move to an option followed by a press of the Enter key. You can also use the keyboard to select an option by pressing the key that corresponds to an underlined letter. The following sections examine each of the Control Panel dialogs in detail.

*Figure 6-4: The Settings Menu.*

**Colors** The Windows desktop uses a standard default color scheme that you have already observed: medium blue title bars and borders for windows, a cream color background for the client area of an application window, and muted grays for just about everything else. These default colors are not your only choice. Windows provides 10 other color schemes that you can choose to give your screen more or less color than the default. If you cannot find a scheme that suits you, you can create your own scheme from a palette of available colors, or even create custom colors to expand that palette.

To replace the Windows default color scheme, choose the Color dialog from the Windows Control Panel to bring up the dialog box shown in Figure 6-5. Click on the arrow to the right of the words "Windows Default" to drop down a small menu offering a variety of other color schemes. The available color schemes are as follows:

- Windows Default
- Arizona
- Bordeaux
- Designer
- Fluorescent
- Monochrome
- Ocean
- Patchwork
- Rugby
- Pastel
- Wing Tips

*Figure 6-5: The Color dialog box from the Control Panel.*

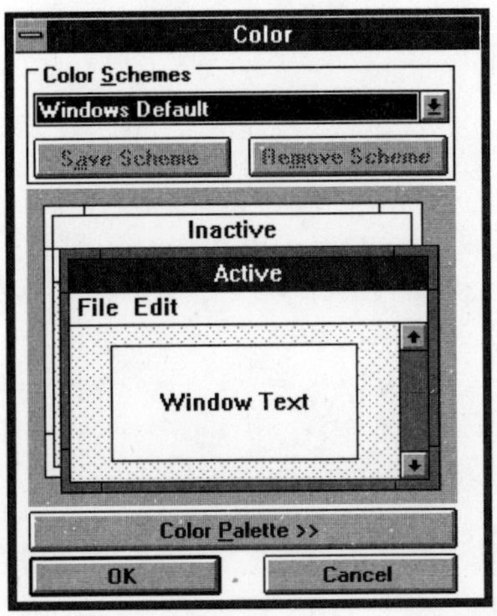


You can scroll through the names of these schemes. While you scroll, the colors of that scheme change the look of the small sample window inside the Color dialog box. As you can see, the choices vary from the sedate (Monochrome, Ocean, and Wing Tips) to the flashy (Fluorescent, Patchwork, and Pastel) with a few more in between. To adopt one of these schemes, choose the name of the scheme you like best and click on the OK button or use the keyboard arrow keys and Enter to make a choice.

You can experiment with one or all of these schemes to see how you like the "new" look of Windows. You can change to another scheme any time you wish, and you can go back to the default color combination whenever you desire. When you choose a new color scheme, Windows saves the new scheme in a special file called WIN.INI; Chapter 7 discusses this file in more detail.

Should none of the offered color combinations appeal to you, you can create your own custom scheme. With the Color dialog box open on your screen, select the button labeled "Color Palette." This selection increases the size of the Color dialog box and displays the palette shown in Figure 6-6 (shown here in black and white.) The small boxes on this palette contain 48 colors you can use to create your own window-color scheme.

*Figure 6-6: The palette from the Color dialog box.*

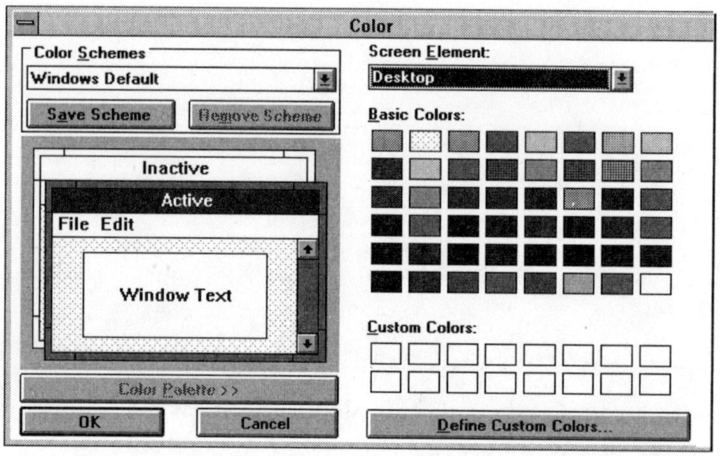


Creating a custom scheme involves choosing the portions of the sample window whose color you want to change. Click on the title bar and notice that the words "title bar" appear in the box labeled Screen Element. You can also click on the arrow icon to the right of this box and drop down a list of all the parts of the screen whose colors you can change. The screen elements whose colors you can change are the following:

- Desktop
- Application Workspace
- Window Background
- Windows Text
- Menu Bar
- Menu Text
- Active Title Bar
- Inactive Title Bar
- Title Bar Text
- Active Border
- Inactive Border
- Window Frame
- Scrollbars

Play with different color combinations to get a feel for creating your own color scheme. When you hit upon a combination you like, press the Save Scheme button near the upper-right corner of the Color dialog box. When you choose to save your scheme, another dialog box appears to let you enter a name for this new color scheme. When you provide a name, Windows saves this color scheme and adds it to the Color Schemes list.

The 48 basic colors provided by the color palette do not limit your choice of available colors. You can specify custom colors by pressing the button marked Define Custom Colors. When you press this button, the dialog box shown in Figure 6-7 appears. This new dialog lets you create custom colors by manipulating the small arrow icons to the right of the boxes that contain numbers; these boxes carry the labels Hue (which is a measure of the mixture of primary colors), Sat (for saturation, the intensity of a color), Lum (for luminosity, the lightness or darkness of a color), Red,

Green, and Blue. You can increase or decrease the values in these boxes by pressing the up or down arrows beside them. As you do so, you will see a crosshair on the rainbow-colored display in the large box. The values in the little boxes correspond to the color you see under the crosshair. When you obtain the shading you want, press the Add Color button to insert that color into the Custom Colors palette area in the main Color dialog box. These custom colors can now be used in a custom color scheme.

When you finish making alterations to your color scheme, press the OK button to return to the Windows desktop.

*Figure 6-7: Defining custom colors.*

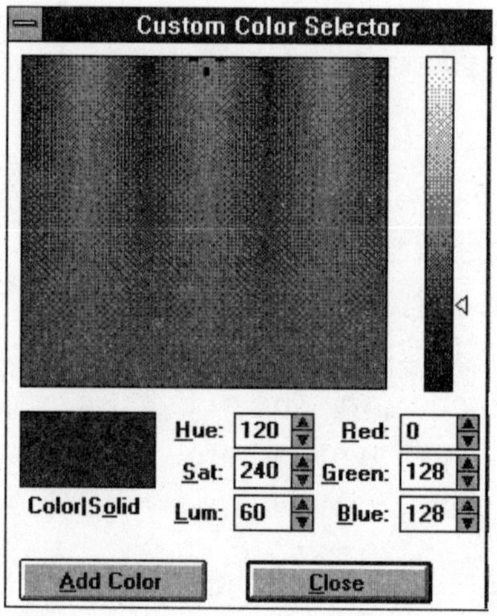


**Desktop** Changing colors affects the color scheme of the various components of a window. To change the look of the large, mostly-empty background screen of windows (the desktop), you can use the Control Panel's Desktop dialog. This dialog lets you modify the background's look, lets you overlay that background with some "wallpaper," lets you establish spacing between icons, lets you control the grid that positions icons and windows, allows you to adjust the width of window borders, and lets you alter the speed at which the screen cursor blinks.

Bringing up the Desktop dialog opens the window shown in Figure 6-8. Inside this window you will see five boxes that allow you to change the desktop's Pattern, Wallpaper, Cursor Blink Rate, Icons, and Sizing Grid. You can leave the dialog without making changes to any of these desktop properties by pressing the Cancel button.

*Figure 6-8: The Desktop dialog box.*

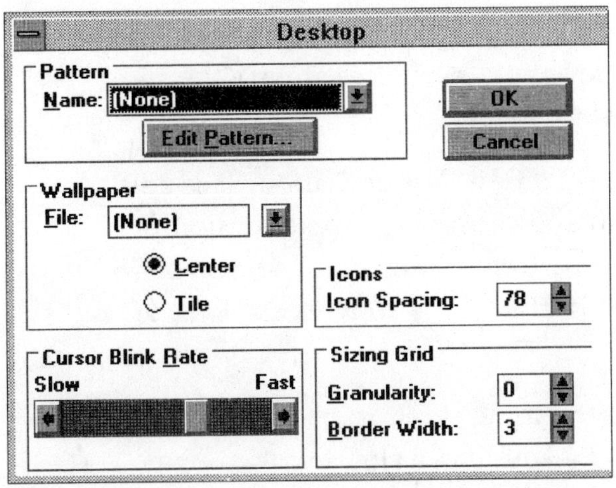


The Pattern option lets you alter the look of the desktop background. You may have already changed the desktop's color; now you can modify its look by adding a pattern to it. Clicking on the arrow icon to the right of the box marked Name drops down a menu of pattern choices. These choices are shown below:

- None
- 50% Gray
- Boxes
- Critters

- Diamonds
- Paisley
- Quilt
- Scottie
- Spinner
- Thatches
- Tulip
- Waffle
- Weave

You can scroll through the choices and choose one, as you did with color schemes using the previous Control Panel dialog. When you press the Desktop dialog's OK button, Windows redraws your screen with the selected pattern in place as your new desktop.

You can also edit a pattern by pressing the Edit Pattern button. This action opens another small window that shows the basic pixel design of the individual graphic that makes up a pattern. In this window, you can then turn pixels on or off with mouse button clicks to alter the look of this graphic and the resulting pattern.

Windows also lets you place wallpaper on the desktop background to provide something more interesting to look at than a simple color or pattern. Wallpaper on the Windows desktop would be analogous to a pictured blotter on a physical desktop. Several bitmaps are available for you to use as wallpaper, or you can create new bitmaps or use any other bitmap that Windows can read (the Paintbrush accessory discussed in Chapter 5 can create and modify bitmaps). The following are the wallpaper bitmaps Windows offers:

- None
- Boxes
- Chess
- Paper
- Party

- Pyramid
- Ribbons

Wallpaper bitmaps can be tiled to cover the entire desktop, or centered to occupy just a portion of the desktop surface. Figure 6-9 shows the Windows desktop with the Paper bitmap displayed as wallpaper. Note: Using wallpaper does decrease the amount of memory available to your applications by from 9K to 150K.

Altering the screen cursor's blink speed merely involves moving the slider bar within the scrollbar that appears under the Cursor Blink Rate label. You can move the slider bar with the mouse pointer (hold down the mouse button and move the mouse) or by clicking on the arrow icons at either end of the scrollbar.

*Figure 6-9: The paper bitmap as wallpaper.*

Icon Spacing refers to the distance on the screen between the icons of running tasks. If you have a large number of tasks running at once, you may discover that icon spacing becomes an issue; if the icons are too close together, reading the labels beneath them gets progressively more difficult. This problem becomes particularly acute when you have many instances of the same application running with different documents; labels become your only way to tell one task from another.

Finally, Desktop lets you adjust the invisible screen grid that underlies the desktop display and the width of window borders. The invisible screen grid controls how windows and icons line up on the screen display. When the value beside the word Granularity is zero, the screen grid is turned off. Setting this value to a non-zero number (using the arrow icons) sets up a grid that windows and icons will line up on when you move them. Similarly, changing the value in the box beside the words Border Width increases or decreases the width of a window's border. You might want to widen the border of screen windows if you find you have trouble grabbing them with the mouse when you want to change a window's size.

**Fonts** Windows comes with several fonts including Helvetica, Times Roman, Script, Modern, Symbol, and that typewriter standby, Courier. You can easily add other fonts from third-party vendors to Windows using the Fonts Control Panel dialog. You can also use Fonts to remove an existing font.

When you bring up Fonts, a window opens to display a list of the installed and available fonts. Below the list is a box that displays a sample, in reverse video, of the font currently highlighted. Scrolling through the list changes the display in the sample window. The sample display shows not only what the letters of a font look like, but also indicates the point sizes that font makes available.

To add a new font to Windows, press the Add Fonts button. This action opens a dialog box that displays a list of files in the current directory that use the .FON file extension. You can highlight any of these font files to begin the process of adding that file to Windows.

With a currently installed font highlighted, you can press the Remove button to delete that font. Windows then pops up a message box asking if you really want to remove that font, and your Yes or No choice removes the font or leaves it in place.

**Ports** Often, newly installed software requires unique settings for a serial port. The Ports dialog lets you adjust settings for up to four serial communications ports. Most machines have only one or two serial ports, but you can add other ports by plugging cards into the computer's expansion bus. Serial ports are used to attach modems, mice, and other devices to the computer.

When you open this dialog, you see icons representing four ports labeled COM1 through COM4, plus buttons labeled OK, Cancel, and Settings. Clicking either an icon or Settings brings up the dialog box shown in Figure 6-10. Making choices from those offered is straightforward.

*Figure 6-10: The Settings dialog box.*

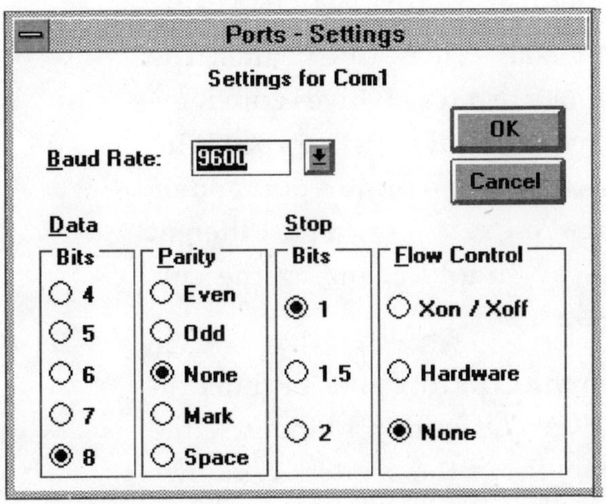


The adjustable serial port settings include baud rate, data word size, stop bits, parity, and flow control (also known as handshaking). The values available for each of these settings, except baud rate, appears beside a check button; clicking a button turns that setting on and any other off. For baud rate, the dialog offers a scrollable menu of choices from 600 to 19,200.

**Mouse** The Mouse dialog permits adjusting the way the mouse attached to your computer performs. The allowable adjustments include the Mouse Tracking Speed, which determines both the area covered by the mouse pointer and the speed at which it moves; the Double Click Speed, which determines how quickly Windows responds to a double-click operation; and, swapping the right and left mouse buttons, a convenience for left-handed mouse users. Increasing the Mouse Tracking Speed enlarges the screen area that the mouse will cover; decreasing this value results in better control of the mouse for fine detail work.

The first two of these adjustments use a slider bar between extremes of Fast and Slow, while switching mouse buttons is a check box option. The Windows default settings for a mouse will be suitable for most people.

**Printer** The Printer dialog lets you add printers to or remove printers from the Windows environment. When you originally installed Windows, the Setup utility prompted you to install at least one printer. The Printer dialog lets you add others. Installing a printer involves copying a device driver for the chosen printer from a distribution disk to your Windows directory. Then, the printer can be assigned to a printer port and be made active by attaching it to that port. You can use many different printers with a single copy of Windows by simply changing the currently active printer using the Printer dialog.

To install a new printer to Windows, open the Control Panel's Printer dialog box (see Figure 6-11). Press the Add Printer button to increase the size of the dialog box and display a lengthy list of the printers Windows supports. Scroll through this list until you find the name of the printer you want to add to Windows. Then, press the button labeled Install. A message box will appear with instructions to put a Windows distribution disk into your computer's A> disk drive. From here, the Printer dialog takes over and adds the new printer to the list of Installed Printers.

*Figure 6-11: The Printer dialog box.*

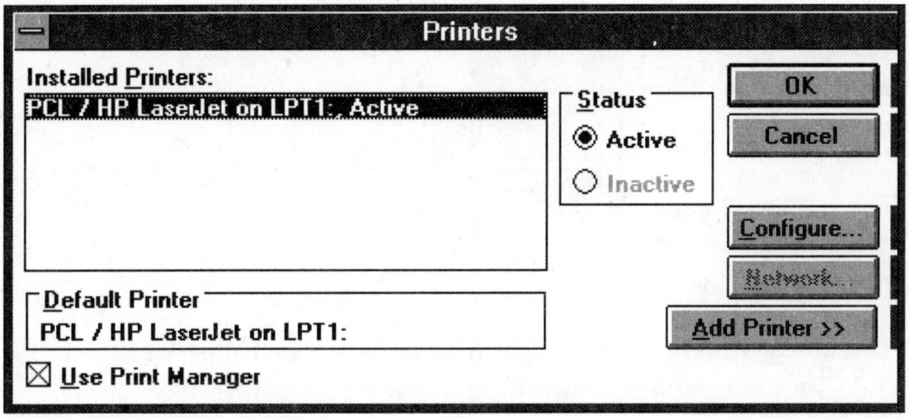


Next, you will need to configure this newly-installed printer. Press the Configure button to display the dialog box shown in Figure 6-12. You next must tell Windows to which port (LPT*n* for parallel, or COM*n* for serial where *n* is a number) the printer will be attached. Two choices on this list, EPT and FILE, refer to a special IBM PS/2 printer adapter card and a disk file, respectively. A section in Chapter 7 explains how to print to a disk file instead of a printer using the Print Manager.

Once you have indicated a port attachment, press the Setup button to make sure the printer's settings are the way you want them, and to help Windows establish which printer you are using (Windows often uses the same printer driver for different models of the same printer). Pressing Setup displays a dialog box similar to the one shown in Figure 6-13; the choices in this dialog box will differ from printer to printer. The box in Figure 6-13 shows the setup choices you can make for a Hewlett-Packard Laserjet laser printer. Each printer will have a series of similar setup options that you can modify. In this example, a single printer driver drives several different HP laser printers; this dialog box lets you tell Windows exactly which printer you plan to use. This dialog box also lets you change settings later if you need to.

*Figure 6-12: The Configure dialog box.*

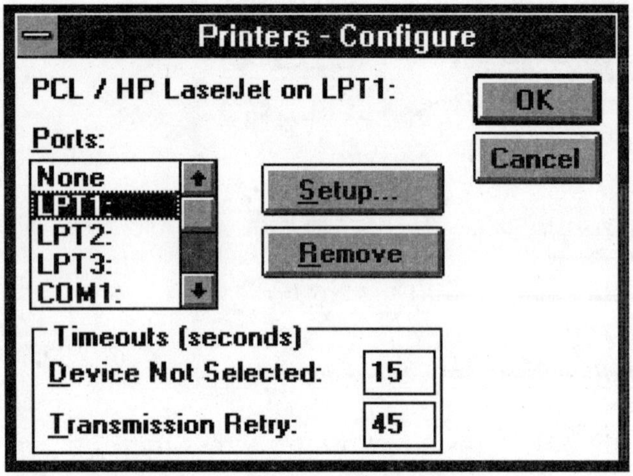


You can print from a Windows application without going through the print spooler called the Print Manager. To do so, you must unmark the small check box in the Printer dialog box labeled Use Print Manager. With no mark in this box, Windows applications will bypass the Print Manager and send printer output directly to the printer port. You will be unable to use your computer during the resulting print operation.

**International** Not everyone using Windows is a North American. Using the Control Panel's International dialog, certain characteristics of Windows can be adapted to use non-U.S. conventions. Table 6-2 shows the many different settings that Windows can use to adapt to non-U.S. usage.

*Figure 6-13: The Setup dialog box for printer options.*

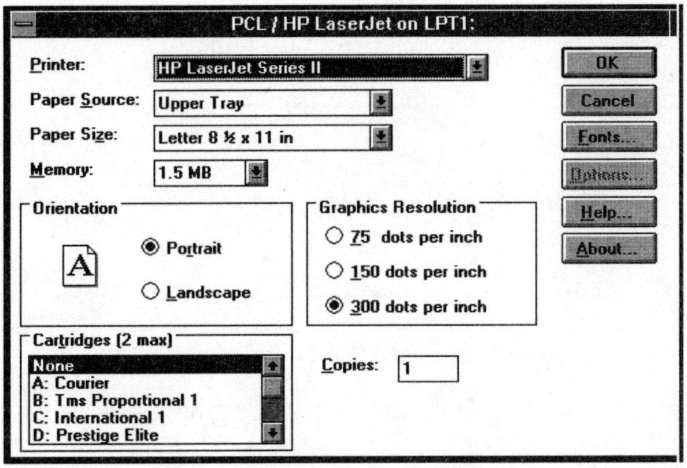


*Table 6-2: Windows choices for country, language, and keyboard layout.*

| *Country* | *Language* | *Keyboard Layout* |
|---|---|---|
| Australia | Danish | Belgian |
| Austria | Dutch | British |
| Belgium (Dutch) | English (American) | French Canadian |
| Belgium (French) | English (International) | Danish |
| Brazil | Finnish | Dutch |
| Canada (English) | French | Finnish |
| Canada (French) | French Canadian | French |
| Denmark | German | German |
| Finland | Icelandic | Icelandic |
| France | Italian | Italian |
| Germany | Norwegian | Latin American |
| Iceland | Portuguese | US |
| Italy | Spanish | Norwegian |
| Mexico | Swedish | Portuguese |
| Netherlands | | Spanish |
| New Zealand | | Swedish |
| Norway | | Swiss French |

| *Country* | *Language* | *Keyboard Layout* |
|---|---|---|
| Portugal | | Swiss German |
| South Korea | | US (Dvorak) |
| Spain | | US (International) |
| Sweden | | |
| Switzerland (French) | | |
| Switzerland (German) | | |
| Switzerland (Italian) | | |
| Taiwan | | |
| United Kingdom | | |
| United States | | |
| Other | | |

The International dialog also lets you modify Date and Time formats to conform to the conventions of non-U.S. locales, and also permits adjusting the format for displaying both numbers and currency. You can also tell Windows to use the metric system for displaying measurements.

**Keyboard** The Control Panel's Keyboard dialog provides a way to control the speed at which characters appear when you hold down a keyboard key. You adjust this speed using a slider on a scrollbar between the extremes of Slow and Fast. The box labeled Test Typematic lets you test the speed you have chosen. The Windows default for this setting is Fast.

**Date and Time** You can adjust both the date and the time settings that the underlying computer system maintains using the Date & Time dialog. Using this dialog lets you adjust the system clock for time changes in the spring and fall caused by daylight savings time, or the date to account for a leap year.

To change either the date or the time, select the part of setting (day, month, year or hour, minute, and second) that you want to modify. Then, type a new figure or click on the arrow icons to increase or decrease the number.

**Sound** Windows warns you by sounding a beep when you attempt an illegal operation. You can turn this audible warning off using the Control Panel's Sound dialog. This dialog box features a check box labeled Warning Beep, which you can check or leave empty to turn the audible warning on and off.

**386 Enhanced** When your computer runs in 386 Enhanced mode (explained in Chapter 3), the Control Panel displays an icon for a dialog box to manage several options that affect this mode (see Figure 6-14). These options deal primarily with two situations: device contention and multitasking when using non-Windows applications.

*Figure 6-14: The dialog box for the 386 Enhanced model.*

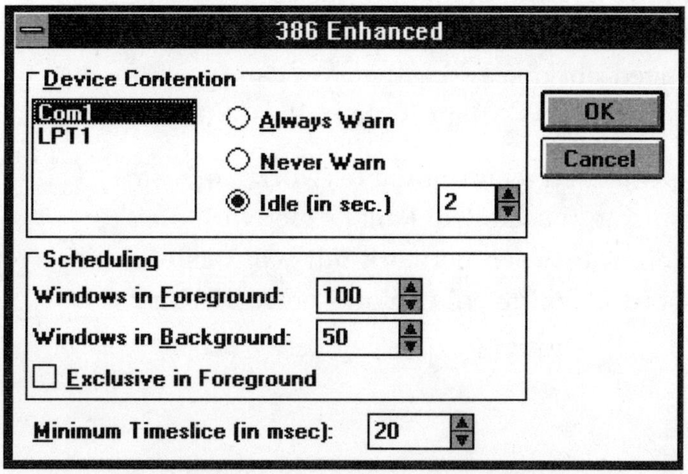


On occasion, more than one program may seek access to a printer or modem at the same time. If these programs are standard Windows application, Windows itself handles the conflict. But when one of the requesters is a non-Windows application, Windows handles the arbitration of the device-access request in one of several ways that users can control from the 386 Enhanced dialog. Table 6-3 lists these options and their effects.

*Table 6-3: Device contention options of Windows running in 386 Enhanced Mode.*

| *Option* | *Effect* |
| --- | --- |
| Always Warn | Causes a message box to pop up any time an application asks to use a device that is already occupied. The box lets the user choose which application gets control of the contested port. |
| Never Warn | No attempt is ever made to prevent clashes between applications, making possible garbled printer output or lost telecommunications data. |
| Idle | Allows the establishment of a time period of from 1-999 seconds; this period is the time that elapses after one application releases a port before another application can use that port without displaying a warning message. |

The other user-controllable option in 386 Enhanced mode concerns multitasking. Chapter 8 explores the issues involved in setting the values for these options. For now, you need only be aware that you can use the 386 Enhanced dialog to adjust the scheduling of multiple tasks.

**Network** When your computer is attached to a running network, you can adjust certain network variables using the Control Panel's Network dialog. These variables will be different for each network but will include options like User IDs and passwords. Chapter 12 explores networks and Windows in more detail.

## Summary

Any of the Control Panel dialogs can be modified at any time during a Windows computing session and the changes takes effect immediately—you do not have to restart the computer. This changeability gives you great flexibility over how Windows performs.

A substantial variety of avenues exist to control the look and feel of Windows. The Control Panel provides the greatest—and easiest—control over colors, the desktop, fonts, and input/display hardware. Chapter 7 presents two other ways to customize Windows.

# CHAPTER 7

# *Customization Using WIN.INI and SETUP*

Using the Control Panel is only *one* of the ways you can modify the appearance and behavior of Windows. Once Windows becomes an integral part of your computing environment, you may want to perform other modifications to it, or set Windows up to start applications automatically. The key to this additional level of control over Windows is an initialization file called WIN.INI.

Both the Setup utility and the Windows Print Manager also provide a great deal of flexibility over the way Windows performs. This chapter explores these tools.

## The WIN.INI File

The WIN.INI file is one of several Windows initialization files. An initialization file is a special file that contains information a program uses to configure itself. (Under DOS, the CONFIG.SYS file is an important initialization file.) WIN.INI contains a variety of settings for controlling the Windows environment. These settings include most of the aspects of Windows that the Control Panel can change—and a few additional ones.

Another initialization file, SYSTEM.INI, contains settings for adapting Windows to customized hardware. SYSTEM.INI is examined in Chapter 11.

The WIN.INI file separates the various settings it uses into the following sections, which are enclosed by brackets in the WIN.INI file itself: windows, desktop, extensions, international, ports, Windows help, fonts, printer ports, devices, and colors. There may also be bracketed sections for applications and Windows accessories like Terminal and Paintbrush. Figure 7-1 shows a sample of a WIN.INI file's contents.

*Figure 7-1: WIN.INI's contents.*

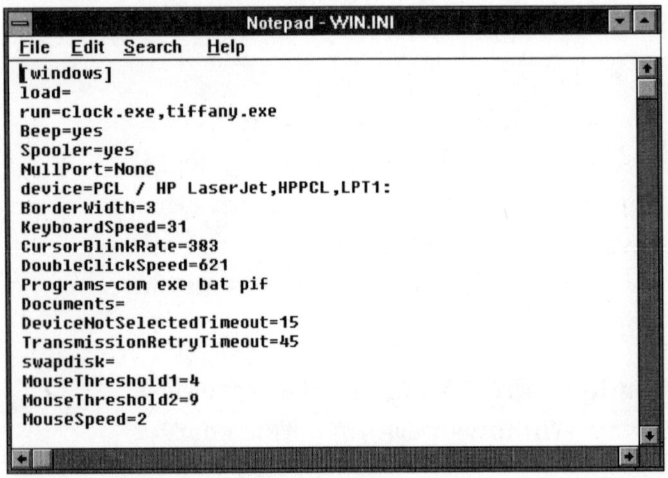


#### *WIN.INI and Its Default Values*

The WIN.INI file does not actually exist until you install Windows. During installation, your choices for printers and ports are incorporated into the WIN.INI file that the installation procedure creates. Most of the settings in the newly-created WIN.INI file are default values. You can use a text editor, however, to change the value of any WIN.INI setting at any time.

Most of the WIN.INI settings can be changed using Control Panel dialogs and, when offered, this method is the safest way to modify Windows. When you make changes to WIN.INI using a text editor, you should keep a backup copy of the original WIN.INI file. Then, should your newly-modified WIN.INI file contain an error that causes Windows to execute in an unpredictable manner, you can restore Windows to its original state.

Each WIN.INI file on a given machine will be unique to that machine and will also reflect the preferences of the last person who modified the Windows environment. After changes have been made to Windows with the Control Panel's dialogs, Windows modifies the WIN.INI file so that the next time Windows loads, the modified environment remains intact.

Table 7-1 lists the settings in WIN.INI that cannot be changed using the Control Panel, and the purpose of each. Each of these settings must be added to WIN.INI, or changed by loading the file into a text editor like the Notepad accessory.

*Table 7-1: Windows parameters that can be changed only by editing the WIN.INI file.*

| *Setting* | *Purpose* |
|---|---|
| Documents=<extensions> | Specifies the files that Windows identifies as document files. Each three-letter extension is separated from the next by a space, and periods are *not* included. Example: `documents=TXT DOC WRI GRP` |
| Load=<filename(s)> | Tells Windows to load a particular application upon start-up and run it minimized as an icon. This value is a list of one or more program filenames, separated by commas or spaces. Example: `load=clock.exe` |
| NullPort=<null-portname> | Specifies the name used for a null port. This name is used in cases where a device is installed (the device driver is present), but not connected to any port. Example: `nullport=none` |

| *Setting* | *Purpose* |
|---|---|
| Programs=<extensions> | Defines the files Windows sees as applications. Extension names are separated by a space and do not include periods. Example: `programs=EXE COM BAT PIF` |
| Run=<filename(s)> | Tells Windows to load one or more applications on start-up and run them in a window. The value is a list of one or more application filenames, separated by commas or spaces. Example: `run=clock.exe, cardfile.exe` |
| WallpaperOriginX=<x-coordinate> | Adjusts the starting pixel location of tiled wallpaper. The default for both the x and y coordinates is 0, making the default origin for wallpaper the pixel location 0,0—the upper-left pixel of the screen. Example: `wallpaperoriginx=30` |
| WallpaperOriginY=<y-coordinate> | (See Above.) |
| <extension>=<executable-filename> | Allows associating one or more file extensions with an application so that clicking on a file with the specified extension launches the associated application. For example, associating the extensions .TXT, .DOC, and .WRI with the application `write.exe` will allow launching that application by selecting a filename containing the specified extension. Example: (the caret ^ symbol functions as a wildcard indicator) `pcx=pbrush.exe ^.pcx` |
| <component>=<red-value> | For certain graphic objects, (ButtonFace, Button Shadow, ButtonText, GrayText, Hilight and HilightText), this setting allows modifications to the color scheme (all other changes can be made with Control Panel). Example: `buttonface=10 45 99` |

The most useful of the WIN.INI settings are load= and run=. These settings let you start Windows with the applications you employ most frequently all ready to use. Run= lets you start those applications in a window while load= starts applications in their minimized state. Make sure you place all the programs you want to start with these settings on a single line separated by commas or spaces. Windows only reads one run= or load= statement from WIN.INI.

The swapdisk= statement in WIN.INI lets you specify on what logical hard disk you want Windows to place its swap files. Windows uses swap files to make room in memory for additional program data, a process explored in Chapter 11.

The initialization files PROGRAM.INI, CONTROL.INI and WINFILE.INI are Windows system files that you should not change. Some Windows applications may modify these files when you install them or Windows may change them when, for example, you add a new applications group to the Program Manager.

The SYSTEM.INI files provides a way to control some of Windows more sophisticated hardware-related features.

## Maintaining Windows with Setup

The Setup program that you used to install Windows provides another way to alter Windows' appearance and behavior. You can use Setup from within Windows or from DOS. Running Setup within Windows lets you inform Windows about changes to the display, keyboard, network, or mouse hardware you are using, and to change the status of a swap file (Chapter 11 provides detailed information about swap files). Running Setup from DOS lets you install device drivers not supplied with Windows, update a previously installed device driver, or change a device driver setting that was not alterable from within Windows.

Setup resides in the Program Manager Main application group. When you run Setup from within Windows, the dialog box shown in Figure 7-2 appears. From the Options menu, you can elect to change any of the devices shown. If you recently hooked your computer to a network, for example, you would need to change the device setting for Network. When you elect to make changes, a new dialog box appears with empty boxes beside the four device categories. Each box has an icon at its right that you can click to see a list of possible choices for that category. You can then highlight a choice to select it.

To run Setup from DOS you must first leave Windows. *Do not* run Setup from the DOS Prompt task. Then type "setup" at the DOS prompt once you have exited Windows. Setup lets you make changes to the keyboard, mouse, and display components for your machine. Most likely, if you are running Setup from DOS after Windows is installed, your purpose is to install a device driver not supplied with Windows. To accomplish this task, select the menu option, Other. Setup will then prompt you to insert a disk containing device drivers. Setup can then display the device drivers available on that disk and allow you to select one for installation.

*Figure 7-2: The Setup dialog box when run from within Windows.*

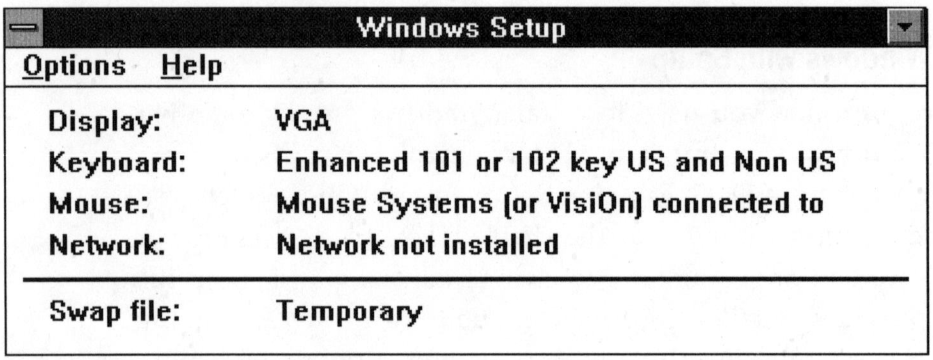


### The Print Manager

While not strictly a way to modify Windows behavior, manipulating the settings of the Print Manager will affect how Windows prints your documents. This section explains how Print Manager works and how to control its behavior.

Print Manager resides in the Program Manager's Main applications group. Print Manager is essentially a user-controllable print spooler through which all Windows applications send printer output. A print spooler is a program that runs in the background to send characters to a printer during the periods when the computer is doing other tasks. Under a multitasking system like Windows, a print spooler is an integral part of the environment. Non-Windows applications cannot use Print Manager and must send printer output directly to the printer, just as they do when running under DOS.

As you print documents from Windows applications, Print Manager creates a *print queue*, a list of files waiting for the printer. Print Manager sends the files in the queue to the printer one after another. You can view the status of the print queue at any time. If you need to speed up printing of a file near the bottom of the list, you can reposition it in the queue.

To the see the print queue, simply open the Print Manager. Any documents in the queue will be listed in the large client area below the menu bar and some print queue controls. The print queue provides information about the printers connected to the computer and the ports they are attached to, and the names of print jobs along with a number to indicate the job's position in the queue. If a print job is working, Print Manager places a small printer icon next to the name of the job. To the right of the print job's name, you will see statistics indicating the size of the file, the time and date it arrived in the queue, and the percentage completed of any currently active print job.

### Controlling the Print Job

Below the menu bar in the Print Manager window, there are three buttons labeled Pause, Resume, and Delete (see Figure 7-3). The first two buttons can stop and restart any printing activity. The Delete button can remove a print job from the queue; the name of a print job below the buttons must be highlighted in reverse video before selecting Delete.

*Figure 7-3: The buttons within the Print Manager window.*

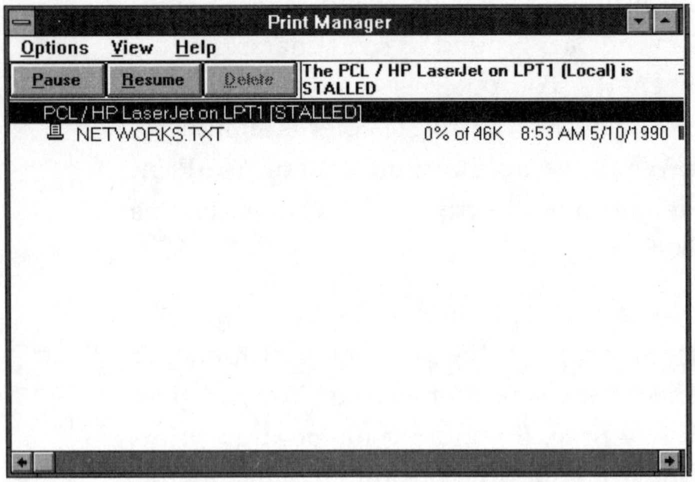


To change the order of print jobs in the queue, simply press and hold down the mouse button while pointing at the name of a print job and drag that name to an earlier position in the queue. Holding down the Ctrl key while pressing the arrow keys is the keyboard method for moving a print job in the queue.

Print Manager has three speed settings for allocating computer processor time to printing operations: Low, Medium, and High Priority. With the priority set to Low, applications run fastest but documents take longer to print. When the priority is High, documents print faster but applications slow down. Medium priority gives print operations and applications an equal share of the computer's processing time.

Print Manager can also control some access to network print queues. Chapter 12 examines the use of Windows with networks in greater detail.

Print Manager also gives you a way to send a print operation to a file instead of a printer. You might want to send a formatted document to a file for later inclusion into another document, or to print it at a later date or on a machine at another location.

To print to a file, you first must go to the Control Panel and engage the Printers dialog. Choose the name of a printer on the displayed list and press the Configure button. In the new dialog box that appears, move to the Ports box and select FILE as the port for printing. When you then exit the Printer dialog, print operations directed to the printer that is now connected to the port "File" will cause Windows to ask for a filename each time you try to print a file. You can also specify a drive and/or directory name along with the filename.

## Summary

Initialization files provide another layer of control for more advanced aspects of the Windows environment. Print Manager provides control over print spooling activity.

With Windows installed and customized to your satisfaction, it is now time to probe the secrets of using Windows to its fullest. Chapter 8 covers application programs and explores how these programs interact with Windows. It also probes the Dynamic Data Exchange facility.

## CHAPTER 8

# *Application Programs and Windows*

Having mastered Windows and the helpful desktop accessory applications that come with it, you will soon want to begin running all your DOS programs from within Windows. As with DOS, there is usually an installation process that precedes using an application with Windows. Once this preparation is complete, however, you can use applications almost as if they were part of Windows itself.

This chapter explores how programs interact with Windows. It explains how to prepare applications for use with Windows, how to use the Program Manager to start an application running, how to keep track of your application programs' use of memory under Windows, and the usefulness of linking applications together to use the same data through a Windows facility called Dynamic Data Exchange (DDE). This chapter also probes the differences between Windows and non-Windows applications and the factors affecting their use.

### The Program Manager

At the center of Windows' ability to run any application is a control accessory called the Program Manager. As you have already seen, the Program Manager is the automatic entry point into Windows—it begins running in a window whenever you start Windows, and closing Program Manager is the safe way to quit Windows.

(See Chapter 11 for an explanation of how you can configure Windows to display another module, like File Manager, instead of Program Manager on start up.)

Program Manager gathers together several classes of built-in programs when you install Windows. These classes, called *groups*, appear as document windows, all or some of which appear as icons in the Program Manager window. These groups include the following:

- The Main group, which includes the Setup, Control Panel, File Manager, Print Manager, Clipboard, and DOS Prompt tasks.
- The Accessories group containing the accessories explored in Chapter 5.
- The Games group containing Solitaire and Reversi.

If there were any application programs on your fixed disk when you installed Windows, there will also be groups for Windows and non-Windows applications in the Program Manager window. The Setup program created these groups during installation. To these, you can add any number of your own groups to organize applications according to your own criteria. For example, you can place a spreadsheet and its ancillary utilities in one group, database tools in another group, and so on. You might even create a temporary group for a particular project in progress. In a later section, you will discover that copying or moving programs from one group to another is an easy operation.

Unless you have a RUN= statement in your WIN.INI file to immediately start running an application, the Program Manager will display an open window on your screen when you first start Windows. See the section on WIN.INI in Chapter 7 for more information about using the run= statement.

The Program Manager window displays the open Main document window the first time you start Windows. Later, when you leave Windows, you can elect to save current settings. This will cause Windows to display whatever Program Manager group window was open on exit the next time you start Windows. To open any other group document window, simply double-click the mouse on its icon or pull down the menu labeled Window and click on the name of a group. Once you have two or more document windows open, you can pull down the Program Manager's Window menu again to select the Cascade or Tile option. The Cascade option instructs Windows to place a newly-opened window onto the screen without completely obscuring the windows beneath it. The Tile option makes Windows place open windows side-by-side as shown in Figure 8-1. An active window may show a scrollbar to indicate that all the icons in that window may not currently be visible. If you subsequently change the size of the Program Manager window or open another group window, you will have to choose Tile again to correctly display tiled document windows.

*Figure 8-1: The Program Manager with four open group windows tiled.*

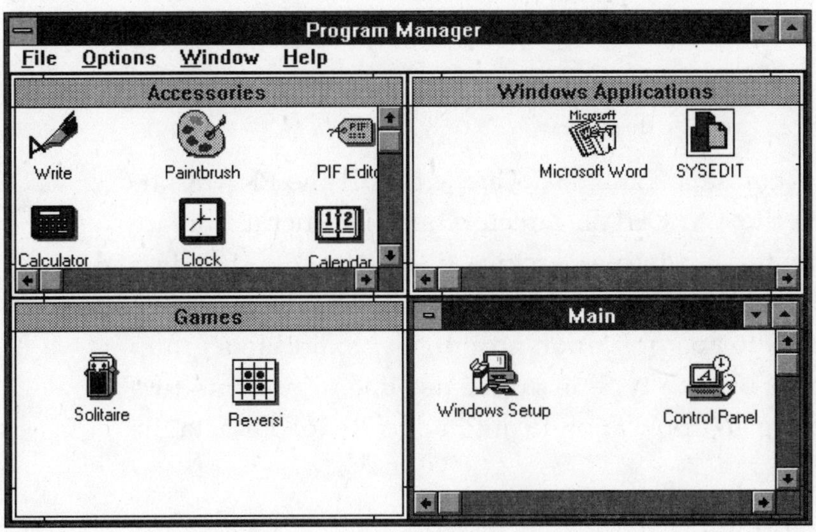

### Starting Applications

The icons in any open group window represent applications that you can start by double-clicking them with a mouse or by pressing Enter when the name under the icon is highlighted in reverse video. Remember, you can move the name highlight bar from icon to icon with the keyboard arrow keys to select an application. Another way to start an application is to choose the Open option from the Program Manager's File menu when an icon's name is selected.

Choosing the Minimize On Use option from the Program Manager's Options menu instructs the Program Manager to shrink to an icon when you start any other application. To get back to the Program Manager once it has been shrunk, double-click on its icon.

If you need to run an occasional application that does not appear in an application group (and you do not want to add it to one), or a program from a floppy disk, you can use the Program Manager's Run option from the File menu. Choosing this option opens the dialog box shown in Figure 8-2. Here, you simply type in the program's path and name and click OK or press Enter. The Run option is one of the ways Windows provides to start an application that requires a variable command-line argument. For example, to start an archive program that requires input and output filenames, you might type

```
c:\archive\pkarc a wp.arc *.doc
```

into the Run dialog's Command Line box. This will start the PKARC archive utility located in the \ARCHIVE directory and instruct it to place all files with a .DOC extension into an archive file called WP.ARC. In a later section, you will discover how to add a program requiring a static command-line argument to an application group, how to add to a group program that requires a user to type in command-line arguments to a group, and how to set up an application to automatically load a data file on startup.

*Figure 8-2: The Run Option dialog box.*

#### Managing Groups

You can add new groups to Program Manager, remove groups you no longer need, and move applications from one group to another. Since including more than 40 programs in a single group is not recommended, you may have to create new groups just to handle the overflow. Furthermore, having programs grouped in some logical fashion helps you use your computer more productively by letting you cluster tasks in the way you normally use them, regardless of how you might store them on a disk.

Groups can use any name you choose although short names use screen space more efficiently. You choose a name for a new group by filling in the Description edit box in the dialog box that appears when you choose the New option from the Program Manager's File menu. To see that dialog box, you first click the Program Group check button in the New Program Object dialog box (see Figures 8-3 and 8-4). You also use this dialog box to provide a filename for the Group file that keeps track of what applications reside in any group; Windows adds a .GRP extension to the name you supply.

You can add a new application to a group in three ways: use the Setup utility, move or copy an application from another group, or use the New option from the Program Manager's File menu to select Program Item as a New Program Object. When you make this last selection, a dialog box for defining the newest member of the group appears. This dialog asks for a Description (the name of the application) and a Command Line. This command line is the full path and filename of the new application. There is a Browse button in the dialog box that allows you to scroll through the .EXE files in the current directory to select a program instead of typing a program's name.

*Figure 8-3: The Program group check box.*

The Command Line box permits you to add a space after the name of the program followed by another filename. This second filename will be loaded as a data file into the application once it is running. For example, the command line

```
c:\windows\editor.exe notes.txt
```

will run the XYWrite program whose filename is EDITOR.EXE and load the NOTES.TXT data file on startup. Clustering applications that load a specific data file on startup allows you to create special groups that hold the data for an individual job. For example, if you were working on an annual report that contained several different pieces of text, a few different spreadsheets, and several separate graphics files, you could group these data files and their applications in a group called Annual Report (see Figure 8-5). Then, any time you needed to work on one component of this report, you would open this group window and select and run the application with the specific data you required.

*Figure 8-4: The New Program Object dialog.*

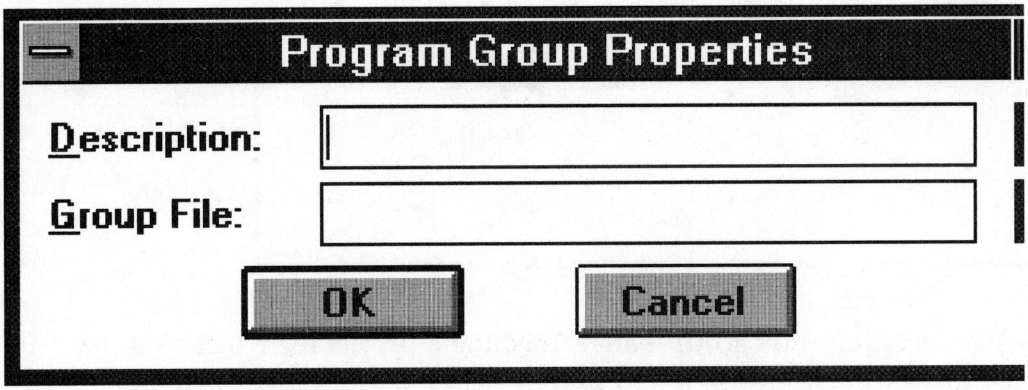


Another way to add an application to a group is to copy or move it from another group. To accomplish this action, you drag the icon you want to copy or move from one open document window to another. You can also drag an icon from an open document window to the icon of another group window. If you press and hold the Ctrl key before you begin dragging, you copy the program to its new destination; without the Ctrl key, you move it to the destination group. Windows will not allow you to drag an icon outside the Program Manager window.

A final way to add an application to a group is to use Setup. Choose the Set Up Applications option from the Setup utility's Options menu and Setup will search all the disks in your computer. Setup then displays a list of all the applications it finds and lets you choose one or more applications to add for use with Windows. When you have chosen them, Setup adds them to the appropriate groups. This method of adding applications to groups works best if you have recently installed several new applications on your machine.

*Figure 8-5: Clustering applications and data files into a project-in-progress group.*

To remove an application group—after finishing a project for which you have set up a special group, for example—select the group so that its name is highlighted and then choose the Delete option from the Program Manager's File menu.

### Keeping Tabs on Memory

A final note about Program Manager: As you open and run applications, the amount of memory free for data and other applications shrinks. Normally, a DOS user keeps tabs on free memory by using the CHKDSK utility. You can run CHKDSK from Windows as long as you do not include the /F parameter, the signal that tells DOS to fix any problems it finds on a disk. But even though you can run CHKDSK, you do not need to use it to find out how much memory is free.

You can keep tabs on how much memory is available under Windows by using the Program Manager's Help menu. The About Program Manager option displays a dialog box that lists free memory in kilobytes and the percentage of available system resources. (You can also obtain this information from File Manager's About message box.) You may have trouble starting new applications if the latter number falls below 25 percent. Later in this chapter, you will learn how the settings in a special configuration file that accompanies an application affects the use of memory.

Program Manager lets you locate and start the many application programs you will use with your computer. Because Windows allows you to run multiple tasks, you will often return to Program Manager to start new applications. The following section explores the kinds of applications you can use with Windows.

## The Types of Windows Applications

Windows classifies application programs as either:

- Windows applications: programs written from the ground up to use Windows user-interface features, or
- Non-Windows applications: programs written without any use of Windows features.

(Under the earlier versions of Windows, non-Windows applications were called *standard* applications.) Each of the two kinds of applications runs successfully under Windows but is treated slightly differently.

Windows applications run in their own separate window and behave just like the Windows accessories explored in earlier chapters. Aldus Corporation's PageMaker and Microsoft Excel are good examples of Windows applications. Windows applications can use the Print Manager to queue the output sent to any printers installed and attached to your computer. They can exchange data using the Clipboard, or by using a facility called Dynamic Data Exchange, which is explored in a later section of this chapter.

Non-Windows applications run full-screen on 8086/88/286 computers instead of in their own window. Lotus 1-2-3 and WordPerfect are good examples of non-Windows applications. Non-Windows applications run about the same speed under Windows as they do under DOS when running full-screen (you may notice a slight degradation in performance because Windows consumes some CPU cycles in the process of managing its ever-vigilant message loop). The CPU (central processor unit) cycle is the amount of time devoted, by the CPU, to the execution of program instructions.

If you run Windows on an 80386 machine, you can run non-Windows applications in their own window. You might first have to set them up to do so by providing Windows with some information about the application. This information resides in a special file called a *program information file* (PIF), explained in detail in a later section of this chapter. Non-Windows applications run noticeably slower when they run in their own window. This performance degradation results from Windows parceling out CPU cycles to any other running applications. You can overcome this slower operation to a large degree on 80386 machines by adjusting the ratio of foreground/background processor time given to an active application. This process is also explained in the PIF section.

Running non-Windows applications in their own window provides many of the advantages of the Windows environment: rearrangeable and resizable windows, the ability to run in background mode and to switch among running applications, and the use of the Windows Clipboard to move data from one application to another.

You can start both Windows or non-Windows applications two ways: add them to a Program Manager group window and then launch them as you would any Windows program; or, choose the Program Manager's Run option from the File menu and type in the application's name as you would at the DOS prompt.

### Windows Applications

A Windows application will remind you of Windows itself. A Windows application was created using a special software development kit that allows programmers to construct application programs from the same building blocks as Windows itself. As a result, a Windows application has menus, windows, dialog boxes, and other features that are identical to Windows.

The only possible problem you may encounter in using Windows applications are conflicts between the 3.0 version of Windows and applications written for earlier versions. You should update any Windows version 1.x or 2.x applications to version 3.0. If an application you want to use is not offering a version 3.0 update, you should run that application under Windows 3.0 *in Real mode only*. If you try to run an application written for an earlier version of Windows under version 3.0, you will be warned by an Application Compatibility Warning message box that running the application may cause Windows to terminate unexpectedly. This message is a polite way of saying that running the application will probably cause your machine to crash and require you to restart the computer, a scenario that will cause you to lose any unsaved data.

Even in Real mode, Windows 3.0 may make older version applications look different: menus and dialog boxes may not display fonts correctly, and the application may not display colors and bitmaps correctly. When you take these factors into account, updating applications for version 3.0 as soon as possible is a prudent course for you to take.

If you have no choice but to run an occasional older version application—which you will run under Windows 3.0 only in Real mode—and also need to transfer data back and forth with version 3.0 programs, use the Windows Clipboard to capture the data to be shared. Then you can save the data to a file and recall it to the Clipboard when you have restarted Windows in another mode. Once recalled to the Clipboard, you can move the data to any other application.

Any Windows application you purchase will provide installation instructions. Once you have installed a new application, you can use Setup or the Program Manager's File menu to add the program to an application group.

### Non-Windows Applications

As a DOS user, you are probably already using several non-Windows applications—programs either purchased commercially or written by someone within your company. You can continue to use those applications with Windows. There are only a few restrictions on running non-Windows applications and these pertain to terminate-and-stay-resident (TSR) programs. Because Windows traps all keyboard activity, most TSRs must be run as stand-alone programs, or they must use a carefully crafted PIF; more on TSRs in Chapter 12.

The choice you must make concerning non-Windows applications is whether to run the application full-screen or in its own window. Running in a window lets you use the Clipboard to exchange data with other applications and allows an application to continue running—recalculating a spreadsheet, for example—even when you switch to another program. Hardware restrictions may make this choice for you. You must have an 80386 or higher machine to run an application in its own window. On 80286 and under machines, you can only run non-Windows applications full-screen and will be unable to share data easily among applications. When you switch from one full-screen application to another, only the foreground application actually runs; all other applications become dormant.

### Program Information Files

On Windows' distribution disks there are a variety of files that have the three-letter extension, .PIF. As mentioned earlier, PIF stands for program information file. These files contain information that lets you use non-Windows applications without having to make any advance preparations beyond installing the application on your computer. PIFs are to application programs what WIN.INI is to Windows and CONFIG.SYS is to DOS. If your Windows distribution disk does not provide the PIF for an application you want to use, check the application's distribution disk; some vendors write PIFs for their applications so that users do not have to. If you cannot locate a prewritten PIF, you can create one using the PIF Editor accessory.

PIFs are not mandatory, however, they are extremely helpful, particularly on 80286 and under machines where fewer options are available for running non-Windows applications. Most programs run fine under Windows without a PIF because Windows makes some basic assumptions about a program's behavior unless told otherwise. If you run a program without a PIF and it does not perform as expected, you should create a PIF for that application. Setup will not identify programs that do not have a PIF as candidates for inclusion in an applications group when you use its Set Up Applications option. You can still manually add programs that do not have PIFs to application groups by using the Program Manager's File menu New option. You can also run programs using the Run option.

PIFs can make your non-Windows applications fit more smoothly in the overall environment of Windows, and they have the greatest impact when Windows runs on 80386 machines. The key to working with PIFs is the PIF Editor accessory.

**The PIF Editor** Found in the Program Manager's Accessories application group, you use the PIF Editor to create new PIFs and to modify existing ones. When you select the PIF Editor icon, a dialog like the ones shown in Figures 8-6 and 8-7 appears (Figure 8-6 is the 386 Enhanced mode dialog; the Standard mode dialog appears in Figure 8-7). To modify an existing PIF, use the File menu to open one of the files with a .PIF extension offered in the resulting dialog box and load it into the PIF Editor. To create a new PIF, simply begin entering information into the edit boxes within the dialog.

Regardless of which Windows operating mode dialog you work with, when you create a new PIF you place the executable filename (the name of the .EXE file) of the target application in the Program Filename edit box. The text you place into the Window Title box will appear on the title bar of the window an application runs in if your machine allows non-Windows programs to run inside a window, and as an icon title. The Optional Parameters box lets you specify any static command-line arguments for starting up an application; a question mark in this box tells Windows to display a dialog box when an application is started to allow the user to type in a command-line argument. For example, if you always started your Quattro spreadsheet with the /x argument to allow the use of extended memory, you would place the /x in the Optional Parameters box. If you want to be able to type in a different argument each time you start the application, type a question mark (?). The Start-up Directory box holds the name of the directory you want to be active for file operations when the application runs. The Memory Requirements boxes provide default values that will be suitable for most applications.

*Figure 8-6: The PIF Editor dialog.*

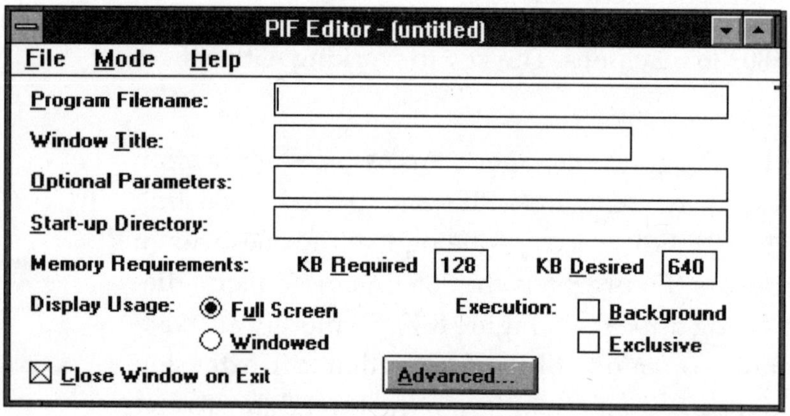


The other choices you can make in the PIF dialog depend on the mode in which your machine runs: The PIF Editor creates different PIFs for 386 Enhanced mode and Standard/Real mode. You press the button labeled Advanced to view the secondary dialog options for 386 Enhanced mode, while the original dialog is open on your screen. Table 8-1 summarizes the choices for 386 Enhanced mode and Table 8-2 defines the Standard/Real mode options. Many of the options in Table 8-1 concern memory usage. Chapter 11 discusses Windows' use of memory in more detail.

*Figure 8-7: The 386 Enhanced mode dialog.*

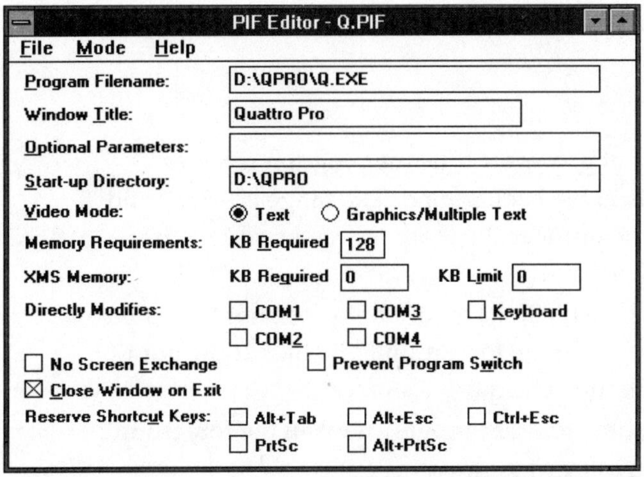


*Table 8-1: The PIF Editor options for 386 Enhanced mode.*

| *Option* | *Action* |
|---|---|
| **Memory Requirements:** | |
| KB Required | The minimum amount of memory needed to run the application; 128K is suitable for most programs. |
| KB Desired | The maximum memory a program might need; the default value of 640K will be fine for most programs. |
| **Display Usage:** | |
| Full Screen | Makes applications use entire screen. |
| Windowed | Runs application in a window. |
| **Execution:** | |
| Background | Allows a program to continue running even when it is not in the foreground. |

| *Option* | *Action* |
|---|---|
| Exclusive | Gives the program complete use of all computer resources while it is the foreground task. No background tasks can execute while an exclusive task is the foreground task. |
| Close Window on Exit | Removes window from screen upon exit. |
| **ADVANCED OPTIONS** | |
| **Multitasking Options:** | |
| Background Priority | The amount of processor time the program receives while it runs in the background. The range is 0-1000 and the higher the number the more processor cycles a background task receives. |
| Foreground Priority | Ranging from 0-1000, the amount of processor time a program gets while in the foreground; the higher the number, the more time it acquires. |
| Detect Idle Time | Gives more time to other programs when the foreground task is waiting for user input. |
| **Memory Options (EMS):** | |
| KB Required | Amount of simulated expanded memory needed to run a program. |
| KB Limit | Upper limit of the amount of simulated expanded memory a program will receive when that memory is requested. |
| Locked | Prevents swapping expanded memory to disk. |
| Uses High Memory | Allows a program to use the first 64K of extended memory. |
| Lock App Memory | Prevents conventional memory programs from being swapped to disk. |
| **Display Options (Video Memory):** | |
| Text | Uses minimal video memory and displays the program in character mode. |
| Low Graphics | CGA resolution graphics for a program. |
| High Graphics | EGA/VGA resolution graphics for a program. |

| *Option* | *Action* |
| --- | --- |
| Monitor Ports | When an application directly manipulates video hardware, allows Windows to correctly restore a program's display. The Text, Low Graphics, and High Graphics settings define programs the same as the Video Memory options above. |
| Emulate Text Mode | Speeds up most applications but should be cleared if text is garbled or the program does not run properly. |
| Retain Video Memory | Prevents running out of memory for applications that switch back and forth between text and graphics modes. |
| **Other Options:** | |
| Allow Fast Paste | An option that should be cleared only for programs that are having trouble pasting Clipboard data. |
| Allow Close When Active | Lets you exit Windows without first closing the program. This practice is dangerous and can lead to lost data. |
| Reserve Shortcut Keys | Transfers the action of keys that normally trigger a Windows action to the application. Check the key combination you want to reserve. |
| Application Shortcut Key | You can define a special key combination to immediately bring a program to the foreground without going through the Task Manager, or cycling through windows. |

*Table 8-2: The PIF Editor options for Standard/Real mode.*

| *Option* | *Action* |
| --- | --- |
| **Video Mode:** | |
| Text | Specifies that a program runs in normal text mode. |
| Graphics/Multiple Text | Specifies that a program runs in graphics mode or uses more than one text screen's worth of video memory. |
| Memory Requirements | KB Required is the minimum amount of memory needed to start a program; the default is sufficient for most applications. |
| **XMS Memory:** | |
| KB Required | Amount of extended memory needed to run a program. |
| KB Limit | Upper limit of the amount of extended memory a program will receive when that memory is requested. |

| *Option* | *Action* |
|---|---|
| **Directly Modifies:** | |
| COM1,COM2, COM3,COM4 | Prevents data loss resulting from contention for serial ports. |
| Keyboard | Informs Windows that a program traps all keyboard output that disables Windows shortcut keys and makes it impossible to switch to another task, which forces you to exit the application to return to Windows. |
| No Screen Exchange | Saves memory by disabling Clipboard operations. |
| Prevent Program Switch | Saves memory by disabling task switching; you must exit the application to return to Windows. |
| Close Window on Exit | Removes window from screen upon exit. |
| Reserve Shortcut Keys | Transfers the action of keys that normally trigger a Windows action to the application. Check the key combination you want to reserve. |

Any time you start the PIF Editor, you will see that some settings have already been set or chosen and others have not. These are the default settings that Windows uses to run applications that do not have a PIF. If you want Windows to use different settings as the default for all applications that do not have their own PIF, you can alter the settings in the PIF Editor and save them to a file called _DEFAULT.PIF. Leave the Window Title option blank but place any valid program name in the Program Filename box; Windows will ignore this file but the PIF Editor must see a filename here before it will let you save a file. You might want to set up a default for Windows that always lets you exit Windows without closing applications, for example.

The power of environments like Windows is that they can let you use a computer like you would use more traditional office tools. For example, you might keep memos to your boss in a separate subdirectory from memos you send to your staff, just as you would store hardcopy memos in separate file folders. The PIF Editor lets you set up several different PIFs for the same application. Using multiple PIFs can let you start up the same application with different active subdirectories, or to automatically load an application with a specific data file. You assign a different name to each PIF you create and place these PIFs in any application group. Then, you can start an application according to the needs of a particular situation.

For example, if you maintain a daily expense report with a spreadsheet program, you could create a PIF that loads the spreadsheet and a data file, say, APREXPS.WKQ. You would first create a PIF called APREXPS.PIF by starting the PIF Editor and entering settings for a new PIF. In the PIF Editor's Program Filename box you would type the spreadsheet program's name (for Quattro Pro, for example, type "\qpro\q.exe"); you would type "April Expenses" in the Window Title box; and you would put the data filename (APREXPS.WKQ) in the Optional Parameters box. Save the PIF with the name APREXPS.PIF. With this PIF added to an applications group, you only have to double-click on the icon showing the name "April Expenses" to bring up both the spreadsheet and the proper data file whenever you want to update your expense report.

PIFs can also be used to run DOS batch files and TSRs. Chapter 12 details how to set up PIFs for these files for use with Windows. Chapter 11 discusses what you can do if you get *out of memory* messages when you run non-Windows applications.

If you run Windows on an 80386 machine, you can alter some of the settings normally controlled by a PIF while an application is running and active. This capability allows you to temporarily boost an application's priority, for example. To change application settings on the fly, open the application's Control menu and choose Settings. The dialog box in Figure 8-8 appears. If the application is running in a window, you can reset it to run full-screen (a short-cut way to accomplish this change to full-screen operation is to press Alt+Enter; press those same keys a second time to return the application to a window). You can also make the application Exclusive or change its priority settings. Making an application exclusive means no time will be taken from the application in order to keep other applications running in the background. An Edit option lets you use the Clipboard to transfer data between this application and any other. A special button lets you terminate the application if it is not executing properly. This last-resort option lets you escape from the application to save any open data files before they are lost. You should restart your computer after terminating an application to prevent DOS and Windows from becoming unstable since the malfunctioning application may have corrupted portions of memory.

*Figure 8-8: Changing an application's settings.*

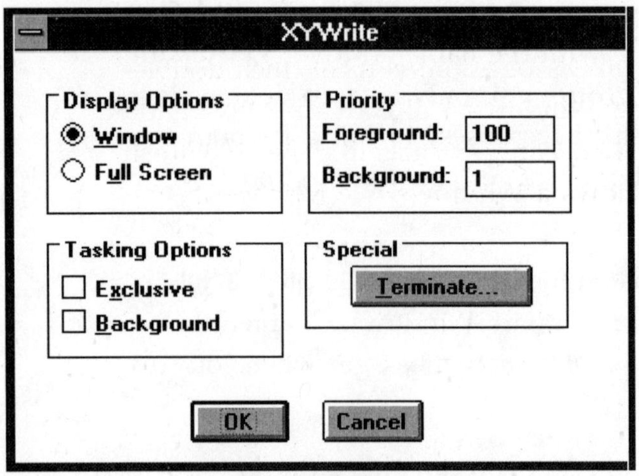


## Getting The Most from Non-Windows Applications

Once you have a number of Windows and non-Windows applications up and running on your computer, you can perform a variety of operations to tune the Windows environment to let you work more productively with your software. You can set up applications so that you can start them by choosing a data file instead of a program. Keeping track of memory usage may become important. And you may need to understand how Windows treats keyboard characters with specific applications.

The following tips will help you get the most out of your Windows and non-Windows applications.

### *Associating Files with Applications*

DOS conventions dictate that certain file extensions—the three-letter combination after the period in a filename—represent certain kinds of files. For example, the extension .EXE means a file is *executable,* and .TXT means the file is a *text file*. Application programs often use their own extension conventions such as .WKQ for Quattro spreadsheet files and .DBF for dBASE III database files.

Windows lets you set up an association between a file extension and an application program. By making this association, you can then double-click on the icon of a data file and Windows will start the application with that data file loaded. In this way, Windows acts like the Macintosh Finder. For example, Figure 8-9 shows a Windows File Manager document window that displays a list of files with the extension .WQ1. These are Quattro Pro spreadsheet files. Selecting any of these files and choosing the Associate option from File Manager's File menu opens the dialog box in Figure 8-10. The name and path for the Quattro Pro program have been placed in the edit box to tell Windows that .WQ1 files are used by the Q.EXE program in the \QPRO directory. Once you push the OK button, Windows will load Quattro Pro when you double-click on a .WQ1 file.

You can associate more than one extension with a single program. For example, earlier versions of Quattro used the .WKQ extension for data files. These files work fine with the Quattro Pro as well. By associating .WKQ files with Q.EXE, you can start Quattro Pro by selecting one of these data files, too. Chapter 7 mentioned a way to associate files and applications in the WIN.INI file, but setting up associations manually is the simplest way.

*Figure 8-9: A Windows File Manager document window.*

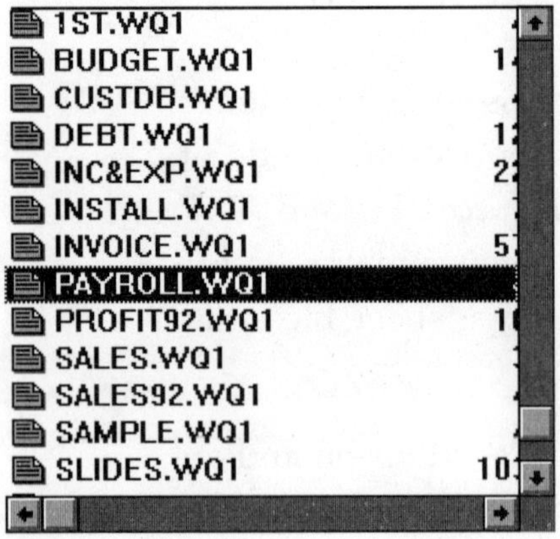


*Figure 8-10: The Associate option.*

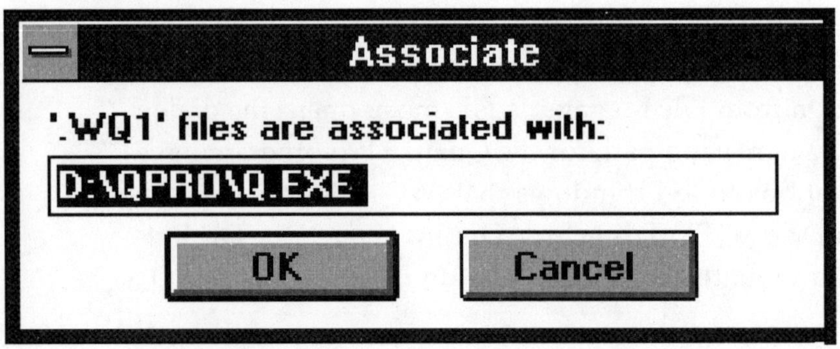


### The ANSI Character Set

Windows supports the American National Standards Institute character set. This character set is slightly different than the Extended IBM PC character set. Windows can display only the IBM PC Extended character set characters that duplicate ANSI characters. You can enter ANSI characters for which there is no corresponding key on your keyboard—the British pound symbol, for example—by typing Alt+0+nnn on your keyboard's numeric keypad (press NUM LOCK to activate the keypad), where nnn is the three-digit code for an ANSI character. The British pound symbol could be entered by typing Alt+0163.

Windows translates IBM PC Extended character set sequences into ANSI sequences on the fly. If you entered the pound symbol by typing the Extended character sequence Alt+156 in a Windows application or accessory, Windows would translate the 156 to the ANSI 163 value. If you subsequently used the file with a non-Windows application, this character might appear as something different. Likewise, any data file prepared by a non-Windows application may contain characters that a Windows application may display incorrectly if those characters cannot be translated to an ANSI equivalent.

## Dynamic Data Exchange

The underlying mechanism that lets Windows handle mouse events even when they occur outside the window of an active application relies on a complex message-passing scheme that you as a Windows user never see. But this mechanism has another use: it allows Windows applications to exchange information behind the scenes. The facility that makes this possible is Dynamic Data Exchange (DDE). DDE is substantially different from Windows other data exchange facility, the Clipboard.

DDE gives you much flexibility in a multitasking environment. The key concept behind DDE revolves around links between application program files. The Microsoft Excel spreadsheet program, for example, can link two separate worksheet files so that a value in one file is linked to and dependent on a value in another file. Other spreadsheet programs can perform similar links between template files but these links are *static*, or unchangeable. Excel can use the Windows message-passing system to make the links between separate files *dynamic*. This means that changing the value in one file automatically changes the affected value in the linked file.

DDE is controlled exclusively through the applications that use it. Excel users create links between worksheets using Excel macros, and links between worksheets and Word documents similarly. From the Windows user's point of view, DDE is never in evidence outside of Excel or Word or any other application that supports DDE.

The DDE facility has many uses. For example, in the Acme Box Company the sales manager must produce a monthly report for the board of directors. Each day, the sales manager receives sales data from several salespeople in the field. The manager enters this data into four separate worksheets covering the regions in which Acme does business. These worksheets in turn are all linked to a database file that is used to compute sales commissions. The original four worksheet's grand total cells also link to a formatted Word document that has been set up to present monthly data in just the way the chairman likes to read the report. This document lists data in tables and also presents it on a graph.

Since all these files are linked together, the sales manager needs to spend virtually no time preparing the end-of-the-month report because he or she has already accumulated the data into the formatted document that will be printed out and taken to the directors' meeting. A manager could also create links over a local area network among worksheet files in different departments to produce a summary worksheet for a branch of a business.

DDE differs from the Clipboard because the exchange of data under DDE is automatic once links have been established. Once linked together, applications share the same data, regardless of which application is being used at any given moment.

DDE can also be used to link a terminal program that might gather stock market data from an on-line service and feed it directly to a spreadsheet template that calculates the worth of a stock portfolio. Similarly, a scientific instrument gathering data on some outside event might be linked to Excel to perform instant analysis of the incoming data.

## Summary

The component central to the operation of Windows application's is the Program Manager. This control accessory organizes applications into groups. Starting an application in a group is a simple matter of choosing and selecting program icons.

Windows runs both applications created to look and operate like Windows itself and stand-alone DOS applications like Lotus 1-2-3 and WordPerfect. Windows often uses a Program Information File to run a non-Windows program properly. PIFs can be created and modified using the PIF Editor accessory.

Applications running under Windows can use ANSI keyboard-control characters. Dynamic Data Exchange lets Windows applications automatically exchange data using links between data files.

The chapters in this section have prepared you to get the most out of your interactions with Windows. In the next section, you will see how to perform the many DOS functions you already know using the many facilities Windows provides. These important functions begin with disk use and directory maintenance.

# PART TWO

# *A DOS User's Survival Guide*

## *CHAPTER 9*

# *Managing Disks and Files*

Acquiring the skills to conquer DOS takes hard work and perseverance. Not many DOS users would easily relinquish their knowledge of DOS arcanum and their mastery of the mysterious C> prompt. For some people, DOS knowledge is like baseball trivia: a way to impress new acquaintances and to further one's reputation around the office. For most of us, however, knowing the ins and outs of DOS is necessary to stay productive. Fortunately, learning DOS has much in common with bicycle riding—once you learn it you never forget it.

Of course, a mastery of DOS provides more than a way to climb the corporate ladder. Knowing DOS means being able to get the most out of your computer. Understanding the nuances of batch files, device drivers, and directory structures can make your work simpler and therefore more productive. Having conquered DOS, why consider using Windows as your access to the computer and DOS? The answer: Windows lets you perform most of the tasks you do with DOS in an easier and faster manner.

This chapter shows you how to use Windows to manage your disks and files. You will discover how Windows streamlines the creation and navigation of directories, how it helps you maintain files, and how it supports disk operations. In short, this chapter will attest that Windows can help you to further your knowledge of DOS.

Windows does not duplicate all the capabilities of DOS. There are many tasks that DOS commands handle more appropriately than Windows. The discussion that follows assumes a familiarity with DOS. Consult your DOS manual or a good DOS book if you do not understand the techniques touched upon here.

## The File Manager

Earlier versions of Windows provided access to DOS through an accessory called the MS-DOS Executive. With Windows 3.0, this control accessory has been replaced by the accessory called the File Manager. The MS-DOS Executive, a file called MDSOS.EXE, is shipped with Windows 3.0 for earlier-version Windows users who feel comfortable with it. This File Manager is an exact duplicate, both in function and appearance, of the OS/2 Presentation Manager File Manager. The File Manager provides a multitude of ways to view and manipulate your computer's disks, directories, and files.

Selecting and starting the File Manager icon from the Program Manager's Main group window displays the screen shown in Figure 9-1. The File Manager task window includes an open document window that displays a *directory tree.* This graphic, similar to the one the DOS TREE command generates, describes the directory hierarchy of the contents of the disk drive whose icon at the top of the File Manager window is highlighted in reverse video. In Figure 9-1 you will notice that the particular computer this display was taken from had two floppy and two hard disks (actually, one hard disk partitioned into two logical drives, C and D). If your computer is attached to a LAN, icons for any active network drives will also appear just below the Directory Tree title bar, as will an icon to represent a RAM drive if one is installed. The free space on the currently selected disk is shown at the bottom of the File Manager window in a *status bar* that can be turned on and off using a check option from the File Manager Option menu. As with the disk drive icon, the root directory at the top of the directory tree is highlighted in reverse video. All other directories are shown as branches off the root directory.

*Figure 9-1: The File Manager's Tree menu.*

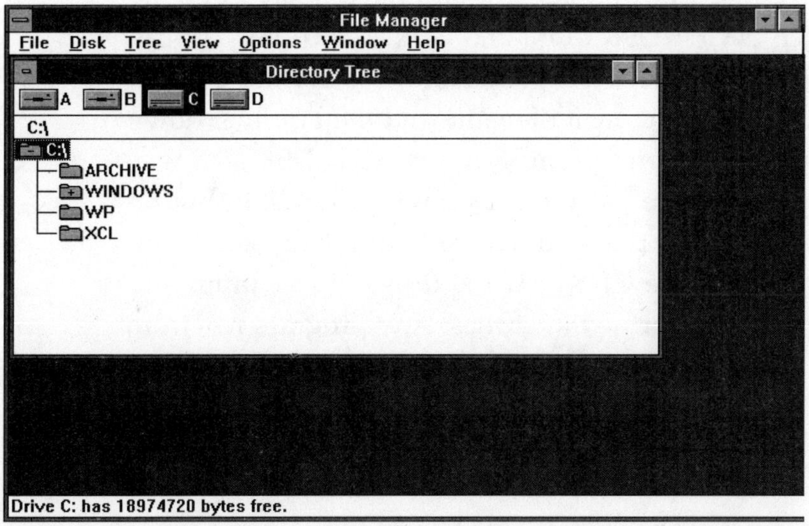


To see the directory of any other disk, you can double-click on one of the visible disk drive icons, or press and hold the Ctrl key followed by the letter of the drive whose disk you want to view. To see a list of the individual files in any of the directories displayed, double-click on a directory's icon, a miniature file folder. File folders that have a plus (+) symbol inside them contain subdirectories; when you click once on such an icon, the directory tree expands to show one or more subdirectories. When a directory has been expanded this way, the parent directory file folder icon changes to display a minus (-) sign; click on the icon again and the subdirectories displayed disappear. This action is called *expanding* and *collapsing* directories. The File Manager's Tree menu offers several options for expanding and collapsing directories without using a mouse.

Double-clicking on any directory icon opens another document window, called a *directory window,* within File Manager and this window displays the files in that directory (see Figure 9-2). The disk drive name and the path for the described files appear in the directory window's title bar area. You will recognize many of the filenames on the display in Figure 9-2 as DOS utilities such as CHKDSK.COM and FORMAT.COM. You can run many (but not all as a later section explains) of these utilities by double-clicking their icons or by selecting a filename and then pulling down the File menu to choose the Open option. Running CHKDSK this way flashes the screen display you are used to seeing with CHKDSK, but returns you to Windows so quickly that you may not be able to read the information. This happens because CHKDSK requires no user input and terminates as soon as it has performed its duties. Any program run from File Manager returns to File Manager when it finishes running.

*Figure 9-2: A directory window.*

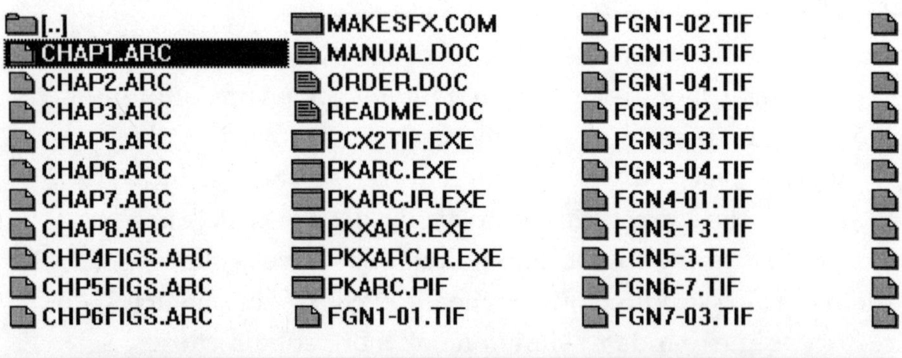


File Manager displays files within a directory window using the file's name along with one of four different icons: a file folder to represent directories, a rectangle with a color bar at the top to represent a program or batch file, and lined and unlined rectangles with a corner folded down to represent document files and all other files, respectively. A rectangle with lines in it means the document file has been associated with an application and can launch that application when double-clicked. You can move to the bottom of a list of files with the END key and back to the top of the list with the HOME key. The PAGEUP and PAGEDOWN keys let you move through the list one page at a time (a page being the number of files that fit in the window).

Once you have an open directory window on the screen, you can use the File Manager's many menus to alter the look and the content of the file displays. The View menu (see Figure 9-3) lets you control the amount of information displayed about a list of files. The default viewing options show a file's name and its type, or three-letter extension, sorted by type. You can use the File Details option to see information about the file's size, the date and time the file was last modified, and the file's attribute information. The Include option opens the dialog box shown in Figure 9-4 to let you type in the DOS wildcard symbol * and a three-letter extension, for example, to view only the files in the directory that have the specified extension. The check boxes within this dialog also permit including or excluding certain kinds of files such as programs or documents. This dialog also lets you choose to view hidden and system files. The system default is to show all files except hidden ones.

Choosing the View menu's By Name option displays the files list sorted by name. The Sort By option lets you choose either Size or Last Modification Date as other criteria for sorting a list of files. The Replace on Open option on the View menu tells File Manager to use the same directory window for subsequent displays, replacing the contents of any currently displayed directory or subdirectory.

*Figure 9-3: The View menu.*

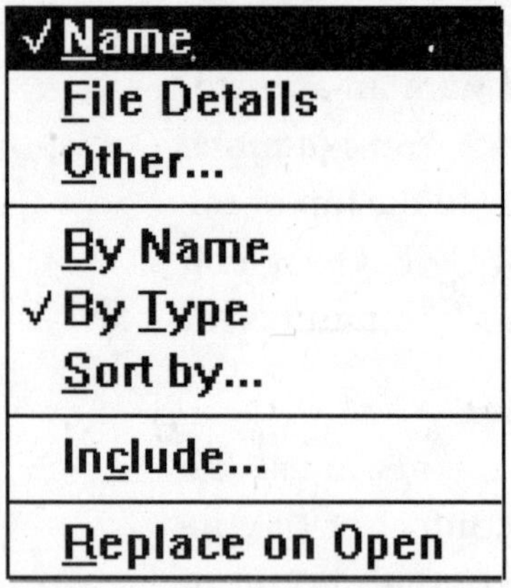


If you choose not to use the Replace on Open option, each directory you view opens another document window within File Manager. You can shrink a directory window to an icon or use its Control menu to close it. You can resize and move a directory window anywhere within the File Manager's window. You can use the Cascade and Tile options from the Window menu to arrange open directory windows on the screen. As you will see in a later section, placing open directory windows side-by-side on the screen can make moving and copying files easier.

*Figure 9-4: The Include option.*

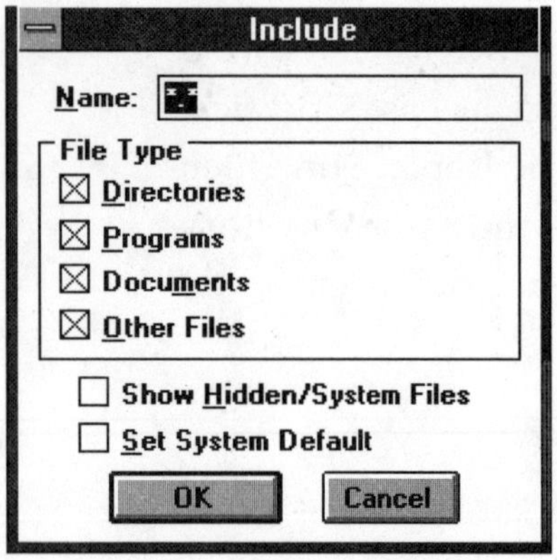

### *A Directory Tree*

DOS users quickly despair at seeing an endless list of filenames scroll by when they command their computer to display the directory of its hard disk. The solution to this problem lies in separating files into logical units. Once separated, you can view files in smaller, easier-to-understand clusters. The principal unit of logical organization under DOS is the directory.

The Windows File Manager not only lets you view the directory tree, or hierarchy, of any disk, but it also allows you to create and delete directories. Under DOS, you would use the MKDIR command to create a directory and the RMDIR command to delete one. To create a new directory under Windows, you make sure the root directory is selected and then choose Create Directory from the File Manager's File menu. (To create a subdirectory, you first select the parent directory and then Create Directory.) This action opens the dialog box shown in Figure 9-5. Here you type the new directory's name into the edit field box and press Enter or the OK button to create the new directory or subdirectory. To delete a directory, you first select its name from the directory tree and then choose Delete from the File menu. Message boxes appear and require you to confirm your intentions. Each file within a directory you select for deletion requires a user confirmation before it gets removed.

*Figure 9-5: The Create Directory dialog box.*

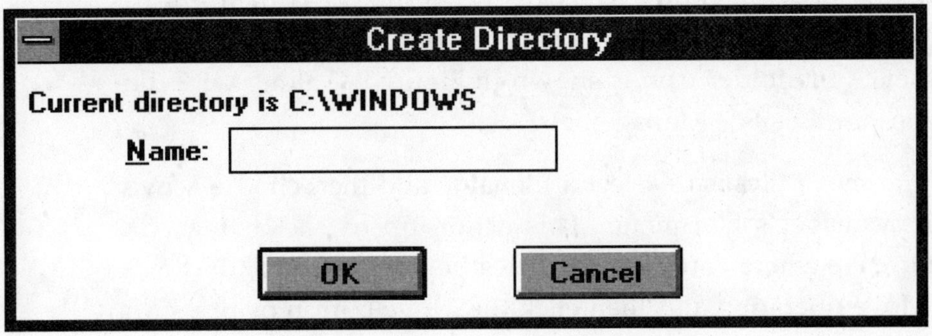

As important as directories and subdirectories are in keeping disks organized, one of the most annoying tasks DOS users face is changing directories. Particularly when a parent directory has several subdirectories, or subdirectories nested several layers deep, typing and retyping the CHDIR command followed by directory names and paths is a tiresome chore. Windows virtually eliminates the need to type the ChDir command and a directory name. As explained in the last chapter, one way to eliminate this chore is to add programs to Program Manager groups; doing so lets you store those programs in any directory but launch them from Program Manager, regardless of the current path. The File Manager also does away with this chore by letting you change a directory with a mouse click. The only occasions where Windows makes you type a directory's name and path occur when you create a new directory, rename an existing one, or add a program to a group.

Another weakness of DOS is its inability to move a file from one disk or directory to another. DOS forces you to copy a file to a new destination and then delete that file from its original location. Windows lets you *move* a file, which combines the copying and deleting actions into a single task.

The simplest way to move a file involves opening and tiling two directories as shown in Figure 9-6. To move a file from one directory to another, you simply drag a file's icon from one directory window to another. Windows places a message box on the screen to let you confirm that you want to make this move operation. You can even move the contents of an entire subdirectory by moving a file folder icon from one directory window to another. A file folder icon is shown in Figure 9-7 along with the other icon types used by File Manager.

Another way to move files is to select a filename and then choose Move from the File Manager's File menu. This action opens the dialog box shown in Figure 9-8 where you type in the destination disk and/or directory for the Move operation and then click the Move button or press M.

To select more than one file for movement, press and hold the Ctrl key while selecting each filename with your mouse.

*Figure 9-6: Two tiled directories.*

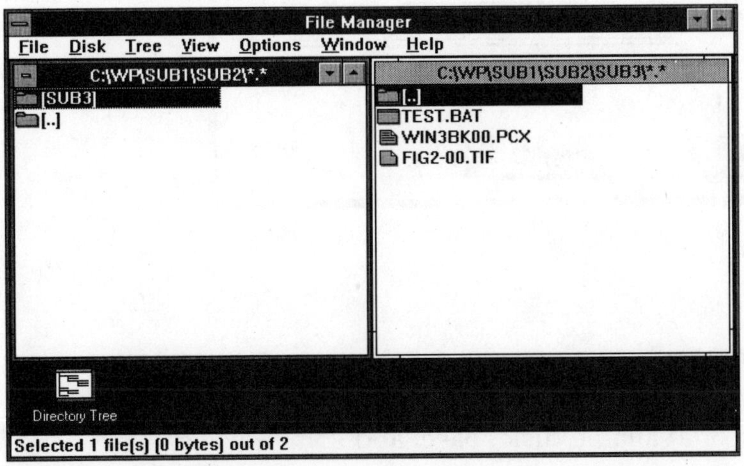


*Figure 9-7: The icons used by File Manager.*

File Manager acts as a control center for disk and file operations. The next section explains exactly how DOS users can use File Manager to perform the disk-related activities they need to accomplish most often.

*Figure 9-8: The Move dialog.*

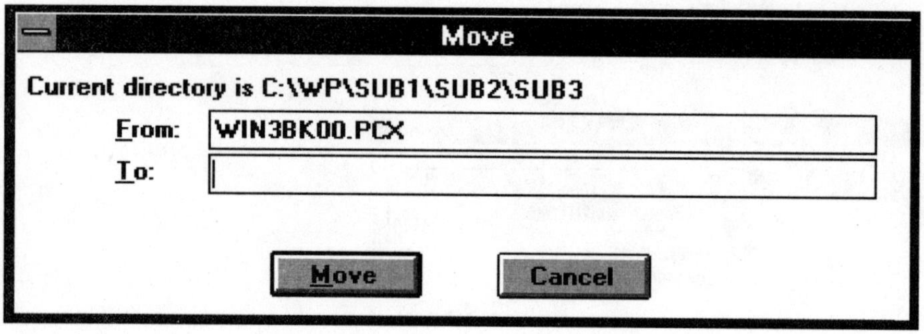


## Disk and File Operations

Directories help you organize disks so you can locate specific data files easily. At a more basic level, you need to prepare and maintain floppy and hard disks, keep track of available disk space, and sometimes compare the contents of two disks. Windows simplifies many of these chores.

For most of the File Manager operations described here, Windows uses two layers of message boxes to let you confirm that the operation you are about to perform is the one you intend. You can turn off the second layer of confirmation message boxes by using the Confirmation option from the File Manager's Options menu. Choosing this option displays the dialog box shown in Figure 9-9. Clicking on any of the check boxes turns off the confirmation listed, since they are all turned on by default. Table 9-1 lists the confirmation options and their corresponding actions.

*Table 9-1: Options for selecting levels of confirmation warnings Windows will issue.*

| *Option* | *Result* |
|---|---|
| Confirm on Delete | Before deleting files. |
| Confirm on Subtree Delete | Before deleting directories. |
| Confirm on Replace | Before writing over an existing file. |
| Confirm on Mouse Operation | Before executing any mouse action that involves moving or copying. |

*Figure 9-9: Choosing confirmation levels.*

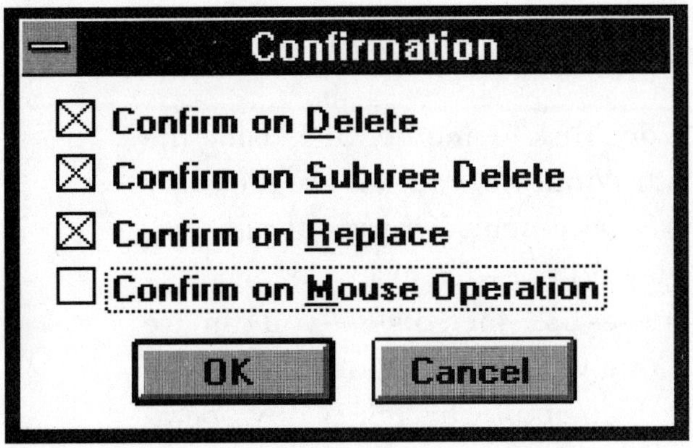


### Disk Operations

Under DOS, you format disks with the FORMAT command. With Windows, the process of formatting disks works similarly. To format a floppy disk, select the Format Diskette option from the File Manager's Disk menu. Windows will display a dialog box asking you to select which disk drive to use for the format operation (if you have more than one drive installed in your computer). Once you have chosen the A or B drive letter, another dialog box appears to let you confirm your intent to format a disk (an operation that removes any data currently on the disk).

When you confirm your intentions, another dialog box appears showing two check box options: High Capacity and Make System Diskette. Placing an X in either of these boxes formats the disk at DOS's highest capacity for the drive type and places the COMMAND.COM file and two hidden system files on the disk. (You can add these system files to an already formatted disk using the Disk menu's Make System Diskette option.) Once the format operation begins, a message box on the screen displays the status of the format operation by showing a percentage completed number (see Figure 9-10). The process takes about the same time it does in DOS, but if you're anxious you can use your computer for other tasks while the disk format operation completes (although your foreground application may slow down somewhat.) When the disk format finishes, Windows displays a message box allowing you to choose whether or not to format another disk.

Under DOS, you copy the contents of one disk to another disk using the DISKCOPY or XCOPY commands. With Windows, you can use the Copy Diskette option from the File Manager's Disk menu *if the source and destination disks have the same capacity*. If they do not—for example, one disk drive uses 3.5-inch disks and the other uses 5.25-inch disks—you can use the Copy option from the File menu along with a "*.*" wildcard designation in the From edit field in the Copy dialog box. This File/Copy operation will copy subdirectories in the same manner as XCOPY. The Copy Diskette operation works best if you use a blank disk as the destination disk; if it is not blank, any files on this disk will be unrecoverable.

*Figure 9-10: Percentage of format completed.*

The Label Disk option on the Disk menu lets you give a disk a name, or label (DOS calls it a *volume label*), or change the label of a disk that already has one. The existing label of any disk is shown between brackets ([..]) in the area just below the disk drive icons within a Directory Tree window. A dialog box with an edit field lets you type or edit the label text for the currently active disk.

The Windows File Manager has no equivalent to CHKDSK. The amount of free space on a disk appears on the status bar at the bottom of a directory tree window. But if you want to know the number of files on a given disk (both hidden and user files), use the CHKDSK command from within a DOS Prompt task; *make sure you avoid the use of the /F parameter.* If you run CHKDSK /F within Windows, you may lose Windows program code or data that may reside in a temporary file that CHKDSK will not recognize.

CHKDSK offers to place any lost data clusters it finds into files for your inspection. If you do not care about this data, answer "no" to the *Convert Found Clusters to Files?* query.

Windows also has no direct way to compare the contents of two disks. You can use the DOS command DISKCOMP from within a DOS Prompt task to accomplish this goal.

### File Operations

The major activity you perform outside an application program—whether under DOS or Windows—is maintaining files: copying, deleting, renaming, combining, and viewing files, among others. These activities under Windows are similar in substance to the equivalent DOS action. What differs is the style of a Windows action. The following sections explore each of these activities in detail.

**Copying Files** The COPY command instructs DOS to make a duplicate of a named file using a specified path to determine the destination of the copying operation. COPY lets you copy the contents of a file to another file of a different name. In the earlier discussion of moving files, you discovered the basics of copying files under Windows. Mouse users can simply press and hold the Ctrl key and then drag any file icon to any visible directory window, icon, or disk icon to copy that file to the intended target. Windows displays a confirmation message box to let you affirm your intentions.

Another way to copy a file is to use the Copy option from the File Manager's File menu. You can select a file for copying before choosing this option. This action opens a dialog box that prompts you to type in the name of the destination disk or directory in the To edit field; the From field will already contain the name of the file you selected. To select multiple files for copying with the Copy option, press the Ctrl key before clicking on a filename or icon; this use of the Ctrl key with the mouse lets you select more than one file. (Remember, selected filenames will be shown in reverse video.) If you do not select a file for copying before choosing the Copy option, the resulting dialog box will have empty edit fields for both the From and To boxes. Having empty edit fields lets you type in wildcard specifications, such as "*.EXE" to copy all program files. Even if text appears in an edit field, you can type over it or press the Backspace key to clear the field.

File Manager also lets you copy a file to a device. To accomplish this action, you type the name of the device in the To edit field in the Copy dialog. For example, to copy a file to a printer, you can type PRN in the To edit field. (The better way to print a file is to use the File menu's Print option with a selected file.) Copying a file to the console device (CON) will temporarily corrupt the Windows display.

Copying and moving files illustrates the one exception to the rule that you cannot drag a file icon outside the File Manager's window. If you want to copy or move a file from File Manager to Program Manager, Windows will allow this action. You cannot drag a file icon to any other window, however.

**Combining Files** Under DOS, you can combine several files into a single file using the COPY command. This operation lets you merge several small files into one larger file, for example. The File Manager File menu's Copy option *does not permit copying multiple files into a single file*. If you attempt this action, Windows protests with a message saying the destination is not a directory.

In order to combine files under Windows, you can switch to a DOS Prompt task and issue a COPY command just as you would under DOS. For example, the DOS commands

```
copy notes1.txt notes2.txt notes3.txt allnotes.txt
```

or

```
copy notes?.txt allnotes.txt
```

tell DOS to merge the files with the five letters "notes" followed by another character and the .TXT extension into a file called ALLNOTES.TXT. This action leaves the smaller files intact.

**Deleting Files** Removing files from a disk under DOS requires the use of either the ERASE or the DEL command. Under Windows, you delete files using the Delete option from File Manager's File menu. You first select one or more files for deletion. Windows then displays a dialog box to confirm that you want to delete the named file. Pressing the OK button or Enter erases the file. Alternatively, you can choose Delete without selecting one or more files and type a filename or a valid DOS wildcard value, such as "*.TXT" into an edit field to delete some target file or files.

**Changing a File's Name** DOS uses the RENAME command to let you change the name of a file and File Manager similarly uses the Rename option on its File menu to perform this operation. Windows uses a dialog box with From and To edit fields for the old name and new name respectively. Any previously selected file's name will appear in the From edit field. You can use DOS wildcards in either of these edit fields to rename a group of files.

**Searching for Files** In spite of your best efforts to organize your disks with directories and subdirectories that will make locating files easier, sometimes you just cannot remember where a specific file might be found. Under DOS, you can only search for files by viewing a directory listing that was generated with some combination of filename characters and wildcard designators. For example, if you wanted to find a file that you knew had the letters "pgmkr" followed by some other characters you could not remember, you could ask for a directory listing in the form

```
dir pgmkr???.*
```

to view all the files in the current directory that have up to an eight-character filename starting with the letters "pgmkr" followed by up to three other characters and ending with any extension. If DOS replied with a *File Not Found* message, you could switch to another directory and make the same request again.

Windows provides a simpler solution to this problem: a way to search the currently active disk drive or directory for single or multiple files. This search operation is engaged from the File Manager's File menu by selecting the Search option. This action opens the dialog box shown in Figure 9-11. You type any valid DOS filename, including wildcard characters, into the edit field in this dialog. You might type the "PGMKR???.*" pattern from the earlier example, or just "*.TXT." The check box in the dialog defaults to search the currently selected logical disk drive, but if you only need to search the current directory, you can click on this box to turn off the entire disk search and therefore speed up the hunt.

Upon completing a disk or directory search, File Manager either displays a message box that says no match was found or it opens a document window with the title Search Results that lists all the files that match the original search pattern, along with their complete path names. You can select any of these files and perform other File Manager operations, such as copying or deleting files. If a file in the Search Results window is associated with an application, you can start the application and load the file by double-clicking the file's icon.

In one respect, the Search Results window is like the Clipboard: it can hold the results of only one search operation at a time. If you perform a search and shrink the Search Results window to an icon, performing a second search replaces the original list of files in the Search Results window with the second search's result and restores the window to the screen.

*Figure 9-11: The Search option dialog box.*

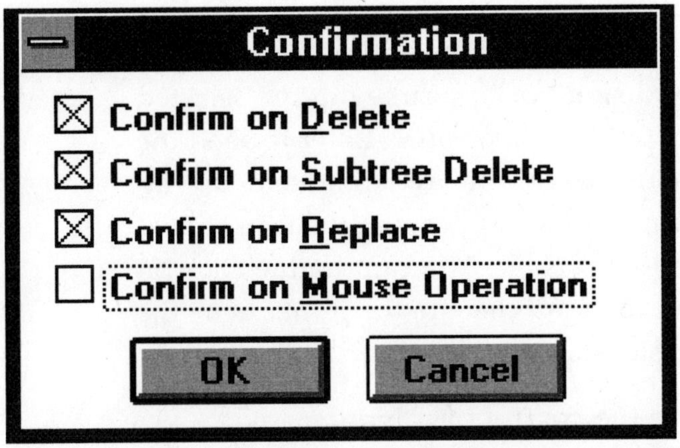


**Viewing a File's Contents** Under DOS, you can view the contents of a file by using the TYPE command. Windows has no equivalent command. But the Windows Notepad and Write accessories can display the contents of any file that contains raw text. You can also use the Clipboard to view the contents of a file; just start or open the Clipboard task and select the Open option from the File menu. If the Clipboard already contains information, you can clear it with the Delete option from the Edit menu. You can also use the TYPE command from within a DOS Prompt task.

**Comparing the Contents of Files** DOS versions 3.0 and later provide the COMP command to let you determine if two or more files are identical. Windows has no equivalent capability. You can issue the COMP command from within a DOS Prompt task to compare two files. COMP takes two arguments, the names of the files you want to compare. COMP returns two kinds of messages: one reports that the files are different lengths, which means they cannot be identical; the other displays the location and different values in hexadecimal format of the two files of equal length.

**Printing Files** DOS provides the PRINT command to let you send files or console activity directly to an attached printer. File Manager provides a File menu Print option for this purpose. You first select a file for printing and then select the Print option (this option stays grayed out and unavailable until you select a file). A dialog box appears with the selected filename in the edit field. Click the OK button or press Enter to send the file to your printer. You will notice that after you have commanded Windows to print the file, the Print Manager icon appears in the icon area at the bottom of your screen if this area is visible. You can double-click on this icon to open the Print Manager to view where in the print queue the print operation you just engaged resides.

Once the Print Manager takes over the control of printing activity, you can switch to it to pause or cancel the print operation. (See Chapter 7 for more information about Print Manager.)

**Setting File Attributes** DOS allows the setting of attributes for files to make those files behave in certain ways. For example, one file attribute makes a file read-only. A read-only file cannot be written to or changed. DOS marks the files which its BACKUP utility creates as read-only. Only by first changing a read-only file's attributes can you make such a file alterable. DOS provides the ATTRIB command for changing a file's attributes. File Manager provides the File menu Change Attributes option for this purpose.

Choosing the Change Attributes option after selecting a file opens the dialog box shown in Figure 9-12. The four check boxes signify the four attribute settings available for any file. The boxes checked apply to the file you selected before choosing this menu option. To change any of these attributes—X in a box means the attribute is on, an empty box means it is off—you simply click on the appropriate box. The attributes and their functions are listed in Table 9-2.

*Figure 9-12: Changing a file's attributes.*

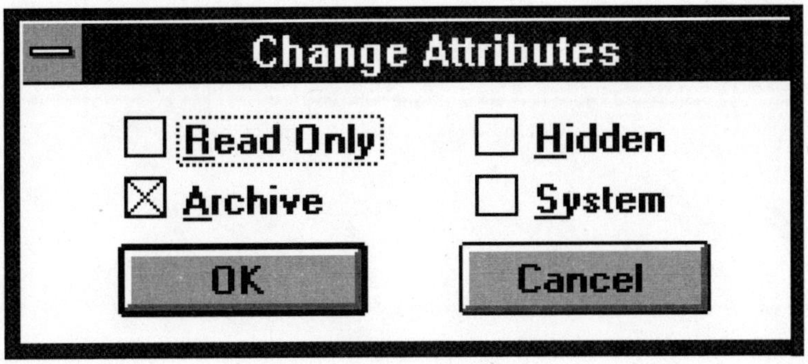


*Table 9-2: The attributes you can set for files.*

| *Attribute* | *Function* |
|---|---|
| Archive | Indicates that a file has been modified. The letter "A" appears in the attribute column in the directory window. It is turned off when you back up your files using DOS utilities such as BACKUP and XCOPY and by some applications. |
| System | Identifies the file as a DOS system file. The letter "S" appears in the directory window. This attribute prevents a file from appearing in directory windows. The file appears only if you have chosen Show Hidden/System Files in the Include dialog box. |
| Hidden | Prevents a file from appearing in directory windows. The letter "H" appears in the attribute column in the directory window. The file appears only if you have chosen Show Hidden/System Files in the Include dialog box. |
| Read Only | Prevents a file from being changed. The letter "R" appears in the attribute column in the directory window. |

## Summary

The Windows File Manager gives you control over your computer's disks, directories, and files. File Manager provides simpler ways to perform classic DOS operations like formatting disks, maintaining directories, copying files, and most other DOS tasks.

In the next chapter, you will see how Windows provides ways to perform less-often-needed DOS activities like backing up disks.

# CHAPTER 10

# *Advanced DOS Functions*

Because Windows is a shell designed primarily to smooth your everyday interaction with DOS, many of the more esoteric DOS functions cannot be performed directly from within Windows. For example, you most likely will not use the BACKUP and RESTORE commands on a daily basis, and commands like VERIFY and REPLACE will get used periodically at best. Tasks like these that you perform only occasionally can be invoked from within a DOS Prompt task under Windows. Starting a DOS Prompt task takes you to DOS while still letting Windows' multitasking kernel manage the computer's memory and thereby keep more than one programming running. Because Windows can run multiple tasks, you can start a DOS operation within a DOS Prompt task and then move on to some other activity while the DOS command does its job.

Table 10-1 shows the Windows operations and the DOS commands that they replace, and it also shows the DOS commands for which Windows has no counterpart. This table also shows the DOS commands that are not necessary under Windows.

The top portion of the table contains commands for which Windows has no equivalent; the bottom lists the Windows operation for performing the given DOS command. The column labeled DOS Prompt contains information about the appropriateness of running the given DOS command under Windows. A "n/a" signifies that the command is not needed under Windows.

*Table 10-1: DOS 3.3 and later command set and equivalent Windows operations.*

| *Command* | *Windows* | *DOS Prompt?* |
|---|---|---|
| append | none | n/a |
| assign | none | n/a |
| backup | none | yes |
| break | none | n/a |
| chcp | none | n/a |
| cls | none | n/a |
| comp | none | yes |
| ctty | none | n/a |
| diskcomp | none | yes |
| disktype | none | n/a |
| exit | none | yes |
| fastopen | none | yes |
| fdisk | none | yes |
| find | none | yes |
| graftabl | none | n/a |
| graphics | none | n/a |
| hsect | none | yes |
| join | none | yes |
| lf | none | n/a |
| path | none | yes |
| prompt | none | n/a |
| recover | none | yes |
| replace | none | yes |
| restore | none | yes |
| set | none | yes |
| share | none | yes |
| subst | none | yes |
| verify | none | yes |
| attrib | File Manager Change Attributes | n/a |

| *Command* | *Windows* | *DOS Prompt?* |
|---|---|---|
| chdir | File Manager | n/a |
| chkdsk | About File/Program Manager | Only without the /F switch |
| command | Windows | n/a |
| copy | File Manager Copy | n/a |
| date | Control Panel | n/a |
| del | File Manager Delete | n/a |
| dir | File Manager | n/a |
| diskcopy | File Manager Copy Diskette | n/a |
| format | File Manager Format Diskette | n/a |
| label | File Manager Labe Disk | n/a |
| mkdir | File Manager Create Directory | n/a |
| mode | Control Panel | yes |
| more | automatic | n/a |
| print | File Manager Print | n/a |
| ren | File Manager Rename | n/a |
| rmdir | File Manager Delete | n/a |
| setup | Control Panel | yes |
| sort | File Manager Sort By | yes |
| spooler | Print Manager | n/a |
| sys | File Manager Make System Diskette | n/a |
| time | Control Panel | n/a |
| tree | File Manager | n/a |
| type | Notepad, Write | n/a |
| ver | About.... | yes |
| vol | File Manager Labe Diskl | n/a |
| xcopy | File Manager Copy | n/a |

To continue to get the most productivity from your computer, you may occasionally find it necessary to perform certain special operations. The sections that follow explain how to accomplish these tasks under Windows.

### Replacing Files

DOS versions 3.2 and later offer the REPLACE command to allow the selective copying of files from one disk or directory to another. Windows provides no similar method of replacing files. You can use the REPLACE command from within a DOS Prompt task to either replace, add, or update files on disks or directories.

### DOS Filters and Pipes

The high-level capabilities DOS provides for redirecting the output of one command or operation to be the input of another has no equivalent under Windows. Like the other DOS commands that have no Windows counterpart, you can use these facilities from within a DOS Prompt task.

### Backing Up and Restoring Disks

Most people perform disk backups at the end of a work day or week. Since backing up an entire hard disk can take up to 45 minutes, this task is best left to a time when the computer is not needed for other chores. At first, the multitasking nature of Windows would seem to lend itself to doing backups in the background with some other task running in the foreground. But BACKUP's monopolization of the computer and Windows use of temporary disk files for swapping program code and data in and out of memory actually makes performing backups while Windows is running inadvisable.

You can perform *selective* backups while Windows is running if you do not mind waiting for BACKUP to finish its operation before you can resume using your computer. The DOS BACKUP command can selectively back up paths, drives, and files. With command-line switches, BACKUP can selectively back up files that have been modified since the last backup, or files that have changed since a given date or time. If you want to perform selective backups of certain file groups—all .TXT or .DOC files, for example—you can perform this chore from within a DOS Prompt task. BACKUP takes over your machine while it runs and makes it impossible for you to switch to another task until it completes its job.

Entire-disk backups are better left as a job you perform after you leave Windows. How you go about the process of backing up a disk depends

upon the mode in which you run Windows. If you run Windows in Real or Standard mode, you can leave Windows and run BACKUP with no further preparation. If you run Windows in 386 Enhanced mode and you have Windows set up to use a permanent swap file, you should change the swap file to temporary before you start your backup. Although changing the swap file from permanent to temporary is not an absolute requirement, a permanent swap file holds no data of any consequence and can be quite large. Leaving it in place will lengthen the backup process unnecessarily. To make this change, you must leave Windows and restart it in Real mode by typing

```
win /r
```

at the DOS prompt. From Program Manager's File menu, select Run. Type "swapfile" into the edit field in the Run dialog box. The Swapfile dialog box appears where you can now check the "delete the current swap file" option. Swapfile will then remove the permanent Windows swap file from your disk. Now you can perform an entire-disk backup.

Even though it is not strictly necessary to back up the Windows program files (since you have the original Windows distribution disks), you should back up any files that have a .INI extension. As pointed out in Chapter 7, these files store configuration information about Windows. In order for Windows to be restored to look the way you have it set up at any given time, the .INI files current for that set up need to be preserved.

Restoring files to your hard disk requires the same kind of approach as backing them up. Selectively restoring files can be done from within a Windows DOS Prompt task. Restoring an entire disk will most likely occur to an empty disk on a machine where Windows will not be running.

### Tricking DOS

Some earlier-vintage application programs require you to place data files on program disks or expect you to use floppy disks for data files when you would rather use a hard disk. Many people get around this restriction by using the DOS ASSIGN command to tell DOS to make a disk drive letter refer to a different drive. For example, ASSIGN B: D: tells DOS to refer to drive B: as drive D: in any disk operations. Similarly, the SUBST and JOIN commands let you treat a directory as if it were a disk, or a disk as if it were a directory. This process can save typing long directory path names.

Most of these reassignment chores will be unnecessary under Windows because Windows seldom makes you type a directory path name. But there is an even more important reason to forego the use of these commands to alter the DOS landscape.

Windows many program modules and accessories expect to find other Windows modules in certain static locations. In addition, Windows uses temporary application swap files under Real and Standard mode, and a virtual memory swap file under 386 Enhanced mode. Altering disk drive assignments and disk and directory names runs the risk of making Windows unstable if it cannot find the files it expects. *Use the ASSIGN, JOIN, and SUBST commands with extreme care.*

## Fine Tuning Disk Activity

Knowing how to use Windows to perform the many necessary DOS tasks for organizing directories and files lets you maximize your productivity with your applications. You may also want to set up your machine to make the performance of all disk drive activity as optimal as possible. The strategies for accomplishing this goal include using a disk cache, using a RAM disk, and making adjustments to your hard disk. The following performance-tuning steps can help make Windows and DOS perform at their best.

### *Caching with SMARTDrive*

A *cache* uses some of the internal memory (RAM) in a computer to hold chunks of information read from a disk. The size of the chunk of information read depends on the size of the cache. If a program—either DOS, Windows, or an application—requests information from disk, the caching utility (which executes like a TSR) first computes whether the requested data is in the cache. If the data is there, it can be supplied to the requesting program more quickly than if that data had to be retrieved from disk. Caching cuts down on disk reads and therefore makes programs execute more quickly.

Windows comes with a cache utility called SMARTDrive that was written to cooperate with the Windows internal memory manager. The SMARTDrive device driver specification gets added to your DOS CONFIG.SYS file automatically upon installation of Windows. SMARTDrive runs each time to start your computer from then on, and significantly enhances the performance of Windows and your applications.

You can adjust the size of the SMARTDrive cache to fine tune the performance of your system. If you add more memory to your computer, for example, you likely will see a benefit from increasing the size of the SMARTDrive cache.

To change the size of the SMARTDrive cache, you must alter your system's CONFIG.SYS file. Use the Notepad accessory to load this file. Then, look for a line that reads:

```
device = c:\windows\smartdrv.sys 1024 256
```

The numbers after the name of the SMARTDrive device driver are the maximum and minimum cache sizes in kilobytes. You can increase the cache size by making the first of these numbers larger. You must restart your computer after you change the CONFIG.SYS file for its changes to take effect. You can experiment with different numbers to find out what values work best with your computer. Larger caches sizes usually produce better performance. This increase is not linear however; increasing the size of a small cache will yield a greater percentage performance improvement than increasing an already large cache.

SMARTDrive runs in extended memory as a default. If your computer is an 80286 computer that uses an expanded memory board, like the Intel Above-board, you can add the /A parameter to the end of the device= command line to run SMARTDrive in expanded memory. You should also make this change if your machine is an 8088/86 computer that uses expanded memory.

#### *Using a Memory-Based Virtual Disk*

In computers that have a lot of extended memory, the only viable use of that memory in the days before Windows 3 was to set up a RAM disk. A RAM disk is simply an area of memory that mimics a disk drive. You can store files on this "virtual" drive, and reading and writing such files happens much more quickly than on even the fastest disk drive. The danger in using a RAM drive is that any loss of electrical power will erase the contents of the RAM disk.

Windows comes with a RAM disk utility called RAMDrive. This utility is similar to DOS's VDISK (VDISK means virtual disk) utility but was created to cooperate with the Windows memory manager. The RAMDrive device driver, RAMDRIVE.SYS, can be found in the \WINDOWS directory on your hard disk after Windows installation. You must add this driver to your CONFIG.SYS file to use the RAMDrive. When you add the following line to your CONFIG.SYS file, Windows automatically creates a RAM disk and displays its icon along with the other disks in File Manager. Use the Notepad accessory to add the line:

```
device = \windows\ramdrive.sys 256
```

to CONFIG.SYS. The number that appears after the driver name reserves that amount of memory for the RAMDrive. You can set this number to any value that you anticipate will satisfy your virtual disk needs. Remember, you must restart your computer after you change the CONFIG.SYS file for its changes to take effect.

The primary use of RAMDrive should be to store any temporary files that your applications might create. If you add the following lines to your AUTOEXEC.BAT file, your computer can use a RAM disk to store temporary files.

```
mkdir x:\tempfiles
set temp=x:\tempfiles
```

(Substitute the name of your RAMDrive for the letter x.) DOS automatically assigns a drive letter name to a RAM drive when the RAMDRIVE.SYS driver is active. Once you have set up this area for temporary file storage, Windows and many applications will automatically place files that have a .TMP extension on this RAM disk.

### *Hard Disk Efficiency*

Windows makes heavy use of the hard disk in any computer on which it runs. Therefore, you need to maintain an efficiently organized disk to allow Windows to run at its best. To keep a disk well-organized requires deleting unnecessary files, removing lost information, regathering fragmented files, and possibly even changing your disk's interleave factor. The purpose of these tasks is to provide as much free disk space as possible. Even if your computer has a 60-, 80-, or 110-megabyte hard disk, you should regularly perform routine maintenance like that described below to keep the disk performing to its capacity.

The steps for maintaining your hard disk include:

- Removing all unnecessary files
- Recovering any lost disk space
- Eliminating fragmented files
- Adjusting the interleave factor

The first three of these tasks can be performed monthly or every other month. Adjusting a disk's interleave factor must be performed only once.

An archiving utility such as PKARC or ARC can make removing a disk's unnecessary files an easier task. Most people are never quite sure if they might need some obscure file at some future date and are therefore reluctant to just delete the file. Using an archive utility, you can place a large number of marginally useful files into a single archive file that you can then store on a floppy disk. Archivers use sophisticated techniques to compress by 50 to 90 percent the individual files that go into an archive file. Place any applications, data files, utilities, or any other files you seldom or no longer use into an archive and you will have them if you need them without cluttering up your hard disk. If you have only a few such files, you can move them to floppy disks without first compressing them with an archiver.

The Windows installation program places a number of files on your hard disk that you may discover you do not need. Table 10-2 lists several Windows files that you can delete or archive to free up space on your disk.

*Table 10-2: The Windows files that many users will never need. Deleting these files adds to the free space on a hard disk.*

| *Filenames* | *Purpose of File* |
|---|---|
| PYRAMID.BMP | A 630-byte bitmap file |
| CHESS.BMP | A 153,718-byte bitmap file |
| BOXES.BMP | A 630-byte bitmap file |
| PAPER.BMP | A 9,662-byte bitmap file |
| PARTY.BMP | A 38,518-byte bitmap file |
| RIBBONS.BMP | A 38,518-byte bitmap file |
| STAR.BMP | A 140,918-byte bitmap file |
| WEAVE.BMP | A 190-byte bitmap file |
| SOL.EXE, SOL.HLP | Solitaire and help file (196,268 bytes) |
| REVERSI.EXE, REVERSI.HLP | Reversi and help file (28,672 bytes) |
| MSDOS.EXE | The MS-DOS Executive (46,640 bytes) |
| PBRUSH.EXE, PBRUSH.HLP | Paintbrush accessory and help (221,290 bytes) |
| WRITE.EXE, WRITE.HLP | Write accessory and help (262,053 bytes) |
| CALENDAR.EXE, CALENDAR HLP | Calendar accessory and help (97,566 bytes) |
| CALC.EXE, CALC.HLP | Calculator accessory and help (62,986 bytes) |

| *Filenames* | *Purpose of File* |
|---|---|
| CARDFILE.EXE, CARDFILE.HLP | Cardfile accessory and help (85,521 bytes) |
| TERMINAL.EXE, TERMINAL.HLP | Terminal accessory and help (191,650 bytes) |
| CLOCK.EXE | Clock accessory (11,136 bytes) |
| EMM386.SYS | Expanded memory simulator (60,946 bytes) |
| RECORDER.EXE, RECORDER.HLP | Recorder accessory and help (68,171 bytes) |
| MSDOS.EXE | MS-DOS Executive (46,640 bytes) |

Grand Total = 1,775,112 bytes, nearly two megabytes.

Occasionally, some data space on a hard disk gets "lost" because the power fails or a user turns off the machine without closing data files. Over time, this lost space can grow to a significant amount. DOS lets you recover this lost space with the CHKDSK command using the /F parameter. *This procedure must be performed outside of Windows.*

As you use a hard disk and work with data files over several work sessions, DOS places parts of the same file on different parts of the disk. This happens because DOS places a new file on the next available space on the disk; if you subsequently go back to an older file and add to it, DOS has no room to place the new data within the space originally allocated for the file. So, DOS places the new data somewhere else on the disk. This process *fragments* files. DOS always knows where the parts of a file are and always maintains the integrity of the file. But it does take more time to read a fragmented file than a file that occupies several consecutive disk sectors.

The solution to the fragmented disk problem requires using a special disk utility that *compacts* a disk. Compacting a disk simply gathers together all a file's fragments into a single contiguous area on the disk. Compacting a disk speeds up file reads and writes.

Like CHKDSK, disk compaction utilities, like the DSKOPT utility that Tandy supplies with its versions of DOS 3.3 and later, must be run outside of Windows. You should also run CHKDSK /F before you compact a disk. Most disk compaction utilities also warn you to back up your disk before you compact it because a power failure in the middle of the compaction process could destroy all the data on your disk.

A more advanced and less often performed disk tuning procedure involves adjusting a disk's *interleave factor*. The interleave refers the placement of sectors on the disk. Depending upon the disk controller, disk sectors that are sequential—that is, sector 2 follows 1, 3 follows 2, and so on—may require a full rotation of the disk before they can be read. If sectors are spaced differently, however, the disk controller can read a sector with only a one-quarter or one-half rotation of the disk, which speeds up disk reads and writes. This spacing of disk sectors is the disk's interleave factor, which is often expressed as a ratio like 3:1 or 4:1.

There are utilities you can purchase that will analyze your disk and readjust the interleave to provide optimum performance. Because the Windows cache program, SMARTDrive reads entire disk tracks into its cache memory, an optimum interleave factor produces the best SMARTDrive performance. Like CHKDSK and disk compaction utilities, a disk interleave adjustment utility should be run outside of Windows.

## Summary

Much of the behind-the-scenes activity of Windows requires maintaining an efficient hard disk. Eliminating unnecessary files and compacting disks can aid the process of providing as much free space on a disk as possible, which allows Windows to run more effectively.

There are several additional factors that affect Windows performance. The next chapter explores how Windows uses memory and other hardware resources.

CHAPTER 11

# *Managing Your Computer's Hardware*

A complex and powerful environment like Windows can put a strain on a computer's hardware resources. Running numerous programs at the same time, printing documents, performing communications tasks in the background, or managing interactions with a network all require that a computer be configured properly in order for these activities to peacefully coexist without bringing the machine to its knees.

This chapter explores how the different resources that make up a computer—principally memory and disks—affect the performance of Windows and its applications. Once you understand how these pieces fit together, you can develop a strategy for setting up your machine to be an optimal Windows performer. This process will revolve around how you use memory, disk swap files, and other computer resources.

## Blueprint of a Windows Computer

The most important components of a computer running Windows are its *total installed memory* and its *usable disk capacity*. As a general rule, the more memory and free disk space your machine has, the better Windows runs. A good deal of memory and disk space means you can run more simultaneous applications and can have larger data files per application, without degrading the performance of any single application.

Windows requires a minimum of 640K of memory to run. The maximum amount of memory it can use is limited only by the amount of extended memory your particular machine can address, or by the amount of expanded memory provided by a card like the Intel AboveBoard. If your machine uses an 80286 processor, you could run Windows in as much as 8 to 12 megabytes of memory. This much memory would allow you to run hundreds of simultaneous tasks. With an 80386/486-based machine, the upper limit could be even higher. For most situations, however, Windows performs quite well with just 1 to 2 megabytes of memory.

Beyond the *amount* of memory in your machine, a crucial performance factor is how that memory is configured. The way you configure memory depends on the type of computer you have, the mode in which you intend to run Windows, and the applications you need to use. Memory configurations depend not only on how much memory is installed in a machine, but also on what software settings and device-manager utilities you use when you start your machine. These settings and managers are controlled by your system's CONFIG.SYS configuration file.

### Types of Memory

The three types of memory found in Intel microprocessor-based computers are:

- Conventional memory, all memory up to 640K.
- Extended memory, any directly addressable memory from 640K to the limit of the processor's addressing range. Requires an extended memory manager like Windows' HIMEM.SYS.
- Expanded memory, banks of memory that are switched into and out of the processor's address range by an expanded memory manager. The most common expanded memory in use today conforms to the LIM EMS (explained below) standards.

Applications have to be designed and coded specifically to use extended or expanded memory.

Windows itself and all its accessories make heavy use of extended memory when it is available. Extended memory is much faster than expanded memory because the computer's processor does not have to perform address recalculations. Windows runs much of its own internal program code in extended memory, which leaves the lower 640K of memory open for running DOS and non-Windows applications that cannot use extended memory. Therefore, the more extended memory that a computer offers, the better Windows runs. Computers that use memory-expansion boards which provide either extended or expanded memory, depending upon how they are configured, should be set up to provide extended memory for Windows.

Using an 8088/86-based computer restricts Windows to real-mode operation only. Windows can use expanded memory in Real mode to enhance the performance of programs only if that memory conforms to the Lotus/Intel/Microsoft (LIM) Expanded Memory Specification (EMS) version 4.0. Windows applications can use LIM EMS 3.2 memory as well, but only to store data, not program code. Windows can use extended memory in Real mode only to store information it would otherwise swap out to a disk.

## Configuring a Windows Computer with CONFIG.SYS

Setting up a computer to run Windows 3.0 requires little effort. The process primarily involves setting up your computer's CONFIG.SYS file with the proper configuration information. The Windows installation program performs most of the required tasks for you automatically.

Everytime you start your computer, it reads a file named CONFIG.SYS. This file contains important information about the memory within your system and about how certain pieces of the system are set up, or *config-*

*ured*. CONFIG.SYS is a text file that can be edited with the Windows Notepad.

Because it is important to provide Windows with as much memory as possible, you should remove from an existing CONFIG.SYS file any device driver load statements that you no longer need. For example, Windows places mouse driver information into its SYSTEM.INI file during installation so you can remove any commands or statements to load mouse drivers from your CONFIG.SYS or AUTOEXEC.BAT files. Similarly, if your current AUTOEXEC.BAT file loads TSRs that you find you no longer need once you start using Windows' many accessories, you should remove them so that they do not load and consume memory unnecessarily. Chapter 12 explains how to use TSRs with Windows.

Being aware of Windows' configuration requirements can help you determine if your machine has been set up properly, and can help you reconfigure your computer after adding new hardware, such as more memory or a new disk drive. The following sections explain how to set up a computer according to the microprocessor it uses. Table 11-1 summarizes the minimum contents of the CONFIG.SYS file that each configuration discussed below should provide.

*Table 11-1: Sample CONFIG.SYS files for different computers.*

| *8088/86* | *80286* | *80386/486* |
|---|---|---|
| **Mandatory:** | | |
| files=30 | files=30 | files=30 |
| buffers=10 | buffers=20 | buffers=20 |
| *EMM.SYS | device=HIMEM.SYS | device=HIMEM.SYS |
| device=smartdrv.sys /a 512 256 | device=smartdrv.sys 512 256 | device=smartdrv.sys /b-1024 512 |
| **Optional:** | | |
| device=ega.sys | device=ega.sys | device=ega.sys |
| | *EMM.SYS | EMM386.SYS |
| 3rd-party device drvr | 3rd-party device drvr | 3rd-party device drvr |

* = the name of the device driver for the expanded memory board being used.

### 8088/86 Computer Set Up

In this day and age, you most likely will run Windows on an 80286/386 machine. But you can run Windows on an 8088/86 machine provided it has at least 640K of conventional memory and as much LIM EMS 4.0 expanded memory as possible.

To configure an 8088/86 computer, place the device driver for the expanded memory board into the CONFIG.SYS file after the file= and buffers= statements. Windows always runs better with the supplied SMARTDrive cache. Therefore, the device driver for SMARTDrive should also go into CONFIG.SYS—be sure it appears *after* the expanded memory device driver device= statement. SMARTDrive has to be run in expanded memory on an 8088/86 computer so the /A parameter appears after the device=smartdrv.sys statement. The size of the cache you can use depends on the amount of expanded memory you have. The minimum useful cache size is 256K, which is the default value Windows will use if you do not provide one. The EGA.SYS device driver is a special Windows device driver that Windows uses to keep track of EGA video registers when you use non-Windows applications in Real or Standard mode.

A later section in this chapter explains how to start Windows with command-line arguments that provide greater control over the way Windows uses expanded memory.

### 80286 Computer Set Up

Computers that use an 80286 frequently come with a minimum of 1 megabyte of installed memory configured as 640K of conventional memory and 256K of extended memory (the remaining 256K is reserved for system use). These machines can also use expanded memory boards for applications that require this kind of memory.

To configure an 80286 computer, first set up any configurable memory boards to provide as much extended memory as possible and to provide only as much expanded memory as any application that uses this memory will need. Place the HIMEM.SYS extended memory manager into the CONFIG.SYS file if Windows installation did not already do so. Next comes the device driver for an expanded memory driver (see Table 11-1). The device= statement for SMARTDrive comes next, followed by the EGA.SYS driver.

### *80386/486 Computer Set Up*

On 80386/486 machines, Windows can use virtual memory if there is at least 2 megabytes of memory installed, and can emulate expanded memory in extended memory. Because of this ability to emulate slower expanded memory, you should set up any configurable memory boards to provide all extended memory.

To configure an 80386/486 computer, place the HIMEM.SYS extended memory manager into CONFIG.SYS. You can alternatively use other extended memory managers, such as the Desqview QEMM.SYS or Compaq's CEMM.SYS, but they may cause memory conflicts in some situations. If you use applications that need expanded memory, add the expanded memory manager EMM386.SYS (see the later section on special command-line arguments for this driver). Then add the SMARTDrive device driver statement followed by the normal and minimum cache size numbers, and the /b- switch to tell Windows not to double buffer disk I/O; this will improve the system's speed when running in 386 Enhanced mode. You would also use the /v switch here if you chose to use an extended memory manager other than HIMEM.SYS. Finally, add the EGA driver load statement if you plan to use non-Windows applications under Real or Standard mode.

## Advanced Device Management

Windows provides a method for controlling a variety of computer hardware resources through its configuration files. Chapter 7 explored the WIN.INI file and the settings it contains in detail. WIN.INI, you will recall, contains information mostly about the current settings for Windows' screen colors and other "look and feel" options.

Another configuration file, the SYSTEM.INI file, contains a variety of special-purpose settings for the sophisticated management of the hardware of a computer running Windows. Few users will ever have to view or change the settings in this file. No attempt should be made to alter a SYSTEM.INI setting without a thorough understanding of its purpose. This file contains settings to specify keyboard, mouse, network, and serial communications drivers. These settings can be changed by running Windows Setup from within Program Manager. Most of the rest of the settings in this file can be changed only with a text editor like the Notepad accessory.

There are some SYSTEM.INI settings that any Windows user might need to change. For example, the default setting for Windows on startup is to open and display the Program Manager. But you can change this default setting to set up Windows to open the File Manager or any other Windows module instead. The shell= statement controls the Windows startup module. Changing the setting in SYSTEM.INI from

```
shell=progman.exe
```

to

```
shell=fileman.exe
```

will cause Windows to open and display the File Manager window when you first start Windows.

Table 11-2 shows a sampling of SYSTEM.INI settings that an everyday Windows user might occasionally need to change. There are a great many other settings that only an experienced computer professional would alter. Information about all the SYSTEM.INI configuration settings is available in several text files that Setup adds to your hard disk when you install Windows. To view these files and learn about other configuration settings, use the Notepad accessory to read any files with "SYSINI" in its filename.

*Table 11-2: A sampling of commonly changed SYSTEM.INI settings.*

| *Setting* | *Purpose* |
|---|---|
| Shell=<filename> | Specifies the Windows program module that runs when you start Windows. Unless you change this setting, Program Manager will run when you start Windows. |
| Swapdisk=<drive-colon- directory> | Provides the name of the disk drive and directory to which Windows swaps non-Windows applications when running in Real or Standard mode. |
| MaxPagingFileSize=<kilobytes> | Specifies the maximum size (in kilobytes) for a 386 Enhanced mode temporary swap file. |
| MinUserDiskSpace=<kilobytes> | Tells Windows under 386 Enhanced Mode how much disk space (in kilobytes) to leave free when creating a temporary swap file. You would want to use this setting if your system's paging drive has less available space than Windows can use for paging. This setting has no effect if a permanent swap file exists. |
| MouseSoftInit=<Boolean> | Specifies whether Windows should reset the mouse hardware. Leaving this switch enabled allows you to use a mouse with a non-Windows application that you start in a window. Disable this setting if you are having problems (extraneous display output or a distorted cursor) using the mouse with an application. If you disable this setting, you will not be able to use the mouse with a non-Windows application that you start in a window. |

| *Setting* | *Purpose* |
|---|---|
| PagingDrive=<drive-letter> | Specifies the disk drive where Windows in 386 Enhanced mode will allocate a temporary swap file. This setting is ignored if you have a permanent swap file. If you don't have a permanent swap file and no drive is specified or the specified drive does not exist, Windows will attempt to put your temporary swap file on the drive containing your SYSTEM.INI file. If the specified drive is full, paging will be disabled. |

### Controlling Expanded Memory

If you run Windows in Real mode with applications that do not require expanded memory, you will set up your machine without any expanded memory. If this description matches your use of Windows, skip the following two sections on using special settings to manage expanded memory.

When you run Windows in Real mode using LIM EMS 4.0 memory, you can control whether Windows uses that memory in *small-frame* or *large-frame mode*. You can also control where the EMS *bank line* is located in a large-frame mode memory frame. A bank line is the dividing line between EMS global memory (available to all applications) and banked memory (available to a single application).

Under Windows, using the small-frame mode is more efficient for running a single, large Windows application. This mode also works best when only a small amount of conventional memory is available. You can start Windows in Real mode with a special argument to use the EMS small-frame mode by using the following command line:

```
win /r /e 999
```

This command line tells Windows to start in Real mode (/r) with EMS small-frame memory (/e 999). The number after the /e is required to tell Windows how much conventional memory must be available to use large-frame mode. By specifying a number that can never be available, 999, Windows will use the small-frame mode. If you load Windows in Real mode without the /e argument, it automatically uses EMS large-frame mode.

The bank line can be moved up and down in memory by loading Windows with the /l argument followed by a negative or positive number. The number represents the distance in memory in kilobytes that the bank line will be moved: -6 means 6 kilobytes down, +12 means 12 kilobytes up, for example. The full command line for adjusting the bank line might appear as follows:

```
win /r /l +10
```

This command line loads Windows in Real mode (/r) and adjusts the EMS bank line (/l) upward by 10 kilobytes (+10). Trial and error is your best bet for determining the best location for the bank line according to the way you use your Windows applications.

### Controlling Simulated Expanded Memory

When running on a 80386-based computer, Windows can provide simulated expanded memory in extended memory through the use of the EMM386.SYS utility. Placing this driver into a CONFIG.SYS file, followed by a number, configures a computer with that amount of emulated EMS memory. For example, the command line

```
device=emm386.sys 512
```

sets up a computer to use 512 kilobytes of simulated expanded memory. The default value for the amount of memory, if no number appears at the end of the command line, is 256 kilobytes.

For special needs, there are numerous optional ways to configure emulated EMS memory. The documentation that comes with your applications will explain any special EMS configurations you may need to set up. Table 11-3 lists the options available for the Windows EMM386.SYS emulator. You would add the appropriate option after the number that specifies the amount of EMS memory. For example,

```
device=emm386.sys 512 w=on frame=D000
```

sets up EMS memory of 512 kilobytes with Weitek processor, a numeric coprocessor similar to an 80387, support turned on (w=on) and the base address of a 64K page frame at hexadecimal address D000.

*Table 11-3: The EMM386.SYS options for configuring simulated expanded memory.*

| *Option* | *Function* |
|---|---|
| w=on/off | Turns on and off support for the Weitek numeric coprocessor. Off is the default. |
| frame=address | Sets a base address for a 64K page frame. Necessary only when a memory conflict occurs. Example: `frame=D000` |
| pn=address | Where *n* is a page number from 1 to 9. Defines the address of a specific page, as in p1=C000. Use of the frame option precludes the use of page numbers 0 through 3. |
| x=address range | Excludes a particular range of memory from use as an EMS page, as in x=E000-EC00 |
| b=address | Marks the lowest address to be used for an EMS page. The default is 4000h. To move the lower bound up to 8000h, use b=8000 |
| l=minXMS | Reserves a specified amount of extended memory before allocating EMS memory, as in l=1024, to make sure that a megabyte of extended memory remains available after EMS memory allocation. |
| a=altregs | Sets the number of register sets for EMS memory. The default is 7 and the range is 0-254. Example: `a=16` allocates 16 register sets. |
| h=handles | Sets the number of handles EMS memory can use. The range is 1-255 and the default is 255. Example: `h=127` limits handles to 127. |

## Disk Space and Swap Files

Free disk space is crucial to efficient Windows operation because Windows uses special disk files, called *swap files*, to temporarily hold program code and data so that computer memory can be made available to other applications and tasks. Windows uses swap files only when the computer's memory becomes too full to allow a new application or task to run.

When running in Real or Standard mode, Windows uses *application swap files*. These files hold code and data from non-Windows applications. Any time you switch to another task from a non-Windows application, Windows swaps all or part of the non-Windows application's code from memory to a disk-based swap file. When you switch back to that application, Windows brings the contents of the swap file back into memory. Windows removes any application swap files from the computer's disk when you leave Windows.

In 386 Enhanced mode, Windows exploits the 80386 microprocessor's virtual memory capability and uses one large swap file for all swapping operations. This swap file can be temporary, which ensures that it will be deleted when you leave Windows, or permanent. Permanent swap files provide several performance advantages over temporary swap files, a subject explored later in this chapter.

### *Application Swap Files*

When you run Windows in Real or Standard mode, starting up a non-Windows application opens a hidden application swap file. This file will not appear in a File Manager directory listing unless you choose a View setting to show hidden files. Any application swap files currently open will be listed with a filename that begins with the four characters "~WOA" followed by several unique characters.

Windows opens application swap files automatically. A Windows user can control only the location of the these application swap files. Because swapping information from memory-to-disk and back takes time, you should instruct Windows to place application swap files on your fastest disk drive, if you have more than one. The SYSTEM.INI file has a setting to control the location of application swap files. Windows will default to using the Windows drive and directory for these swap files unless you change this setting.

To change the location of application swap files, load the SYSTEM.INI file into the Notepad accessory as shown in Figure 11-1. Search for the section labeled *[NonWindowsApp]*. If a swapdisk= setting already exists, you can change it to alter the location of swap files. If one does not exist, create one by adding the text

```
swapdisk=x:\dir
```

replacing x with a drive letter and \dir with a directory name. Save the altered SYSTEM.INI file and restart Windows for the new settings to take effect.

*Figure 11-1: The SYSTEM.INI file loaded into Notepad.*

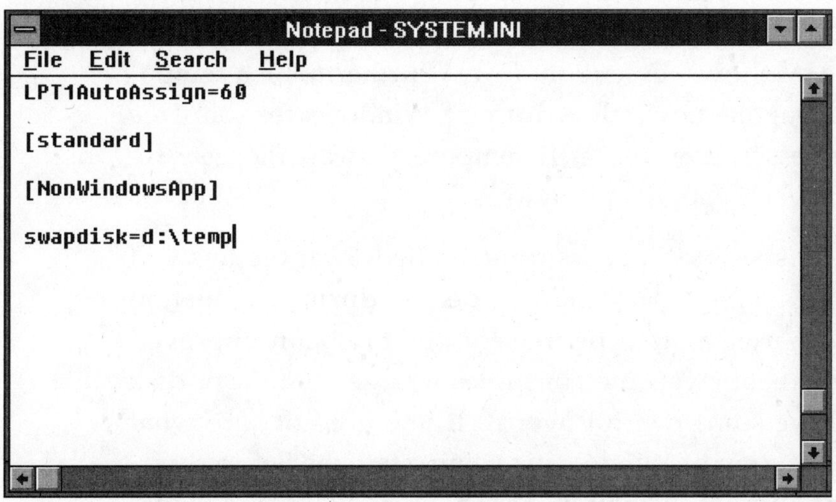

At first blush, using a RAM disk as a swap disk would seem like a good idea since a RAM disk is faster than any physical disk. But Windows removes non-Windows application code and data from memory in the first place to make more memory available for other applications. If your machine's memory space is limited, you probably will not use any of it for a RAM disk. If your computer has a lot of memory, however, using a RAM disk for application swap files will work fine up to the limit of that RAM disk.

Windows removes any application swap files from the designated swap disk when you leave Windows.

### Swap Files in 386 Enhanced Mode

Windows uses one of two kinds of swap file when running in 386 Enhanced mode: permanent or temporary. A *permanent* swap file remains in place on a disk whether Windows is running or not. Permanent swap files use consecutive disk sectors and therefore respond as quickly as possible to swapping read and write requests. A permanent swap file also permits Windows to bypass DOS and directly access the disk, which also increases disk-access speed. A *temporary* swap file must be created anew each time Windows loads and it uses DOS for all disk accesses, each of which slows Windows' execution down. Furthermore, a temporary swap file might fragment over time during a Windows session. This slows down disk accesses even more. A temporary swap file gets removed from the disk when you leave Windows.

**Permanent Swap Files** A special Windows utility called Swapfile lets you change a temporary swap file—the Windows' default during installation unless you specify otherwise—to a permanent one to obtain improved performance. A permanent swap file consumes a large amount of disk space, but you do have some control over it. If you are not sure what kind of swap file your copy of Windows is using, start the Setup accessory and examine the entry at the bottom of the Setup dialog (see Figure 11-2).

*Figure 11-2: Windows Setup shows what type of Windows' swap file you're using.*

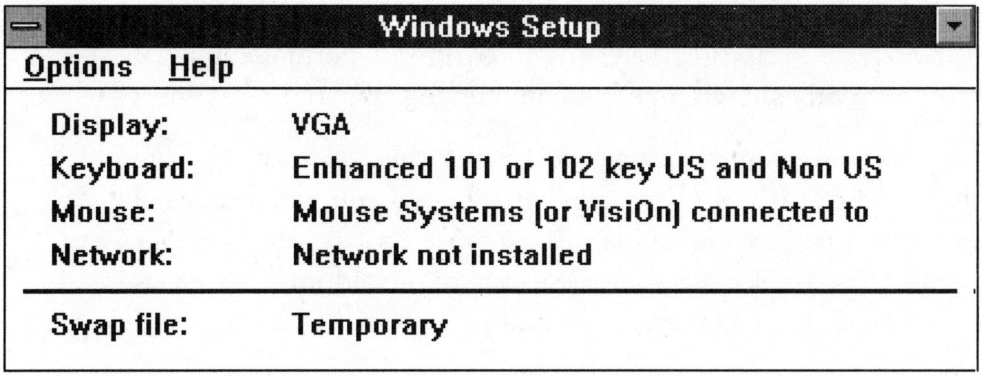


To change the status of a 386 Enhanced mode swap file, you must leave Windows (closing all running tasks first) and restart it in Real mode. As long as Windows is running in 386 Enhanced mode, the temporary swap file is open and active and consumes disk space that could not be used to create a permanent swap file. Therefore, you need to run Windows in Real mode to avoid using any virtual memory swap files. Remember, you start Windows in Real mode by appending the /r switch to the DOS command line entry of "win." Before setting up Windows to use a permanent swap file, you should first compact your disk if you have a compaction utility. A permanent swap file uses consecutive sectors on a disk and a disk littered with fragmented files limits the amount of space available for creating a permanent swap file. (See Chapter 10 for information about compacting a disk.)

Once your disk is ready and Windows is running in Real mode, use the Program Manager's Run option (on the File menu) to run the Swapfile utility. If any other applications are running, Windows issues a message that instructs you to close them down before it can run Swapfile. When Swapfile runs, a dialog box appears that lists the total free space on the currently active disk, and the largest portion of that disk which has contiguous disk sectors available. Finally, Swapfile shows a recommended swap file size in a small box. You can change the value in this box up or down by clicking the mouse on the arrow icons on the right side of the box. Press the Create button or the C key to create the permanent swap file of the size currently shown in the "recommended size" box.

If your computer has more than one hard disk drive, or a single drive with multiple logical drives (also called *partitions*), you can press the Next Drive button or N to have Swapfile report statistics for another drive. You might prefer setting up a swap file on a seldom-used partition, or on a drive that has a faster access time.

Once you have added a permanent swap file for Windows to use in 386 Enhanced mode, any time memory begins getting tight because of the number or size of running applications Windows will swap entire sections, called *pages*, of memory to the swap file. When needed, this information gets retrieved from disk back into memory. The hidden files that use the extensions .SWP and .PAR store the swapped out sections of memory and control information. Do not delete these files or Windows could become unstable.

Should disk space become scarce any time after you have created a permanent swap file, you can remove the file using the Swapfile utility, or use Swapfile to delete an old swap file and create a new one of a smaller size. Once again, you must be in Real mode and have no applications running to call Swapfile. The Swapfile dialog that appears when you have an existing permanent swap file differs from the one you used to create the file. This new dialog has check buttons offering two choices: "delete the current swap file and create a new one" and "delete the current swap file." If you choose to delete one file and create a new one, the original dialog for creating swap files reappears.

**Temporary Swap Files** Electing to use a temporary swap file does not mean giving up control over the 386 Enhanced mode swap file. Windows uses the hidden file WINTEMP.SWP for this temporary swap file and creates this file every time you start Windows and deletes it every time you leave. You can control both the location and the size of this swap file by making adjustments to the SYSTEM.INI configuration file.

The PagingDrive setting lets you control where Windows stores the temporary swap file. This setting resides in the *[386enh]* section of SYSTEM.INI (if no such setting appears in your SYSTEM.INI file, you can simply add it if you need it). The value given for this setting is a drive letter followed by a colon. For example,

```
pagingdrive = d:
```

tells Windows to store the temporary swap file on drive D. If you add a directory name after the drive letter, Windows will keep the temporary swap file in this directory.

There are two other settings you can use in the *[386enh]* section of SYSTEM.INI: MinUserDiskSpace and MaxPagingFileSize. The first of these settings tells Windows how much free disk space you want to have left *after* a temporary swap file has been created. The second setting specifies a maximum size for the temporary swap file. Without these settings, Windows can enlarge or shrink the temporary swap file according to the memory requirements of Windows at any given moment. Windows usually starts out with a 1024K temporary swap file and lets the file grow from there. However, Windows never lets free disk space fall below 500K. If you want to ensure that free disk space never falls below 1024K due to the use of a temporary swap file, for example, you could add the line

```
MinUserDiskSpace = 1024
```

to SYSTEM.INI. To keep the temporary swap file from growing larger than 1586K, use the line

```
MaxPagingFileSize = 1586
```

in SYSTEM.INI. You must save the configuration file and restart Windows for these settings to be used.

Regardless of the size or location of the temporary swap file, Windows removes it from the disk on exit.

## Freeing Up Memory

With Windows' ability to extend DOS by running in protected mode, you will likely see the perturbing message *not enough memory* much less often than you did before. But in those rare instances when this kind of message occurs, there are several things you can do to streamline the way Windows and its applications use memory.

When you run Windows in Real or Standard mode, you can conserve memory with the following steps:

- When you are not using a Windows accessory or application, shrink it to an icon.
- Close applications you will not need to use for a reasonable period of time.
- Make sure the Clipboard is empty by either clearing its contents or saving them to a file.
- Do not use wallpaper to decorate your Windows desktop as these bitmaps can consume up to 150K of memory.
- Alter the PIF memory options for the non-Windows application you are currently using.

If you run Windows in 386 Enhanced mode, add the following techniques to those described above:

- Run non-Windows applications full-screen instead of in their own separate window (use the Alt+Enter keys to toggle between full-screen and windowed operation).
- Alter the PIF memory operations for all the non-Windows programs you plan to use simultaneously.

Together or separately, these steps will provide more memory to your applications.

### *Memory and PIF Options*

When you create Program Information Files (PIFs) for your non-Windows applications, you make assumptions about how those applications will use memory by setting PIF memory options. Most of the time you will use the PIF Editor's default settings. If you later discover that you receive *out of memory* errors when using applications, you can adjust the PIF memory options to make more efficient use of memory.

If you see an *out of memory* message when you try to start an application, edit that application's PIF Memory Requirements: KB Required option by lowering the amount of memory required to run the application. Most of the documentation that comes with applications is vague about exactly how much memory a program needs to run; it may not require as much as the manual indicates. Also, make sure the XMS memory settings for both KB Required and KB Desired are set to zero if the application uses no extended memory. These settings do not affect Windows' use of extended memory, only the application's use of this area.

Another way to provide more memory to an application is to check the Prevent Program Switch option. This option essentially turns the majority of the computer's resources over to the application. You must shut down the application to return to Windows when this option is active. The No Screen Exchange option provides extra memory to an application by preventing Windows from using memory for Clipboard data transfers with the application. Windows also will set aside less memory if you choose the Video Mode:Text option; be sure that your application will not attempt to switch into a graphics mode if you select this option.

When you run Windows in 386 Enhanced mode, the PIF option changes listed above can also help alleviate a memory crunch. There are some 386 Enhanced-only options that can help as well. Selecting the Full Screen instead of Windowed Display Usage saves some memory. The Exclusive option also makes more memory available to an application but prevents other applications from running simultaneously. Making sure the Lock

Application Memory option is *not* selected for other applications also helps keep memory free.

Your last resort, if all these tricks fail, is to add more memory to your computer.

## Summary

Windows runs in different modes depending upon the hardware of your computer and how it is configured. A variety of memory and disk options exist to let you get the most from Windows.

Many options exist for controlling how Windows uses memory. Windows provides several different kinds of swap files to stretch memory and allow more applications to run at once. If memory still gets tight—in spite of swapping and changes to the hardware's configuration—there are several techniques you can use to make applications run more smoothly.

With Windows and many workday applications running successfully, you will next turn your attention to making Windows blend in with the tools that DOS provides for your computer. The next chapter explores this issue, and includes information about TSRs, batch files, and networking.

## *CHAPTER 12*

# *The Merging of Windows and DOS*

While Windows can streamline your day-to-day interactions with DOS, it cannot perform every task you might want to accomplish with your computer. Built-in desktop accessories and multitasking can combine to let you have most of the software at your fingertips that you need to perform the majority of your activities. But there are certain kinds of special-purpose operations that you need to perform occasionally for which Windows does not have a built-in solution.

Many people have come to rely on a group of utility programs to maintain their machine and to help them be productive. For these people, TSRs, batch files, and third-party utilities and applications have become the key to building a useful and productive working environment around a DOS-based computer. After all, there are currently over 10,000 programs that run under DOS to handle the most esoteric of application need.

Windows does not require you to abandon your current investment in these tools. Many of them will work under Windows just as they do under DOS. This chapter explores how to load and run these kinds of special-purpose tools within the Windows environment, and also offers some strategies for dealing with any problems that may arise. The last section of the chapter examines using Windows on a network.

## Memory Resident Software

Many people think DOS has survived as long as it has only because of its ability to support terminate-and-stay-resident (TSR), or memory resident, programs. These programs stay "hidden" in memory until they are brought into the foreground with a special combination of keyboard key presses. Until the arrival of Windows, TSRs were the only way to get DOS to multitask, although this kind of preemptive (or sequential) multitasking is inferior to the true foreground/background multitasking that Windows provides.

Many TSRs run successfully under Windows; experience may prove that some will not (at this early juncture, not many have been tested with Windows 3.0). Because Windows provides built-in accessories such as Notepad, Calculator, Cardfile, Calendar, and others, many people may discover they no longer need their old TSRs. True multitasking will also eliminate the need to use many TSRs since you can easily switch among running applications.

But some tasks, like printing envelopes on your laser or dot-matrix printer for example, may require using a special-purpose program. Networks, too, often require a TSR to watch for incoming network data packets and manage their arrival. When you need to use such a TSR, how you start and run that program will depend on the type of TSR and the way in which it will be used.

TSRs fall into one of two categories: background utilities like screen dimmers or keyboard accelerators, and pop-up utilities like Sidekick.

### *Getting TSRs to Work*

Background TSR utilities function a lot like device drivers and are technically very similar. Background TSRs should be loaded, like the device drivers in a CONFIG.SYS file, before Windows. If you load TSRs this way, they will be available to all Windows and non-Windows applications. You can most efficiently accomplish the preloading of your TSRs by placing the name of any TSR executable file in your AUTOEXEC.BAT file. Chapter 2 discusses how to edit the AUTOEXEC.BAT file.

On occasion, you will want to use a TSR with only one application instead of with all applications. You can load a TSR and an application together by creating a separate batch file that contains the names of the executable files for both the TSR and the application. Then you can use the batch file to start the TSR and the application. You can even create a PIF for the batch file (explained in detail in a later section) to provide some measure of control over how the TSR and the application use computer resources. This technique prevents a TSR from using up memory until you need to use it.

Conversely, pop-up TSRs should be started from within Windows because Windows needs to be aware of their existence. Once started as a separate task, you can switch to the TSR any time you need to use it. You will not need to use its activation keys to make it appear. The TSR will be a running task like any other. You can create a PIF for the TSR as you would for any non-Windows application.

For example, you might run an envelope printer TSR in its own window under 386 Enhanced mode. You would start the TSR using the Program or File Manager's Run option, or you might start it by clicking on its icon in a Program Manager applications group window. Once the TSR's window is open on the screen, you can use it right away or shrink it to an icon until you needed it at some later time. Or, you can simply leave the window open on the screen and switch to that TSR task at any time by clicking on the window's frame to bring it into the foreground.

In Real or Standard mode, TSRs can be run full-screen like other non-Windows applications. The only difference between the operation of a TSR and a non-Windows application is that you sometimes will not be able to switch to another task without first closing the TSR task. A special module, which displays a message box on the screen labeled Microsoft Pop-Up Program Support, may instruct you to enter a Ctrl-C key combination to return to Windows. This action will shut down the TSR, forcing you to reload it to use a second time.

As is always the case with TSRs, experimentation will probably be necessary to see if and how a particular TSR will run with Windows.

## Batch Files and Third-Party Hardware and Software

Batch files under Windows function the same way as under DOS. They use the DOS batch control language and can contain DOS commands. You can use existing batch files and create new ones. You can use the Windows Notepad accessory or the Write word processor (or your own favorite editor) to create or modify a batch file.

Batch files placed into a Program Manager applications group can be started like any application. If a batch file requires some user-supplied command-line input, you can create a PIF for the batch file and place a question-mark symbol (?) in the Parameters edit field box (refer to Chapter 8 for more information on using PIFs).

Figure 12-1 shows the Notepad accessory being used to create a batch file that first displays the contents of a file on the screen and then prints the file. Instructions to the user fall between the "type" and "print" DOS commands. After this batch file is saved, it can be run in one of the several ways that Windows provides for starting applications.

If you use batch files for tasks like backing up or restoring disks, the same caveats that apply to using BACKUP and RESTORE, as explained in Chapter 10, apply to using such batch files.

### *Batch File PIFs*

Creating PIFs for batch files works essentially the same as for any other non-Windows application. Using the PIF Editor accessory, you fill in the appropriate edit fields using the batch file's name and extension and other pertinent information. You then save the PIF and exit the PIF Editor. From that point on, you can use the PIF to start the batch file any time you need it.

The best use of a PIF for a batch file arises when you plan to use the batch file to start a TSR and an application that needs the TSR. Creating a PIF for the batch file allows the setting of any PIF parameters, such as memory and video options, that will affect both the TSR and the application.

*Figure 12-1: Using Notepad to create a batch file.*

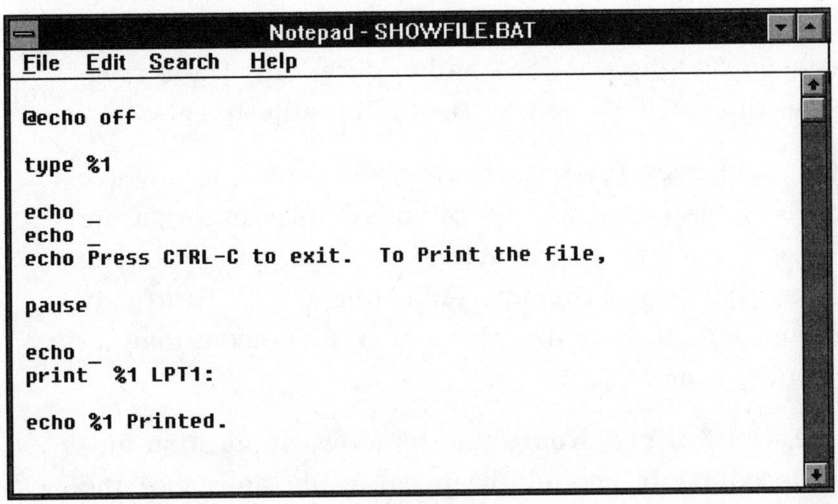


### Hardware and Software Compatibility

Because of the wide variety of hardware that DOS machines have traditionally supported, many new Windows users will expect that they can automatically use video adapters which drive full- and dual-page monitors, for example, or other special hardware. Windows 3.0's design is just different enough from its predecessors to make this assumption tenuous.

Many hardware and software vendors will provide Windows 3.0 versions of device drivers for esoteric hardware. Whether you plan to use the CONFIG.SYS file or batch files like AUTOEXEC.BAT to load special drivers, you should consult with the vendor of any special hardware you use before you install Windows.

As Chapter 9 explained, a Windows computer is still a DOS machine. Therefore, if you have any trouble running a utility or program under Windows, you can simply leave Windows and run the program from DOS as you always have. As time passes, there will be fewer applications that will suffer compatibility problems with Windows.

## When Trouble Strikes

Though unlikely with most applications, you may on rare occasions experience trouble when running Windows and applications. These problems can usually be eliminated with one or two simple adjustments.

The most common problems that Windows users will experience involve non-Windows applications. Losing an application's display, experiencing abnormally slow execution, or being unable to leave an application are all possible with non-Windows programs. Adjustments to PIFs usually solve these problems, although finding the proper adjustment may require trial and error experimentation.

For example, if the screen display from a non-Windows application running in 386 Enhanced mode should disappear, you can revise the program's PIF to select the Monitor Ports option. Some programs bypass the computer's BIOS (Basic Input/Output System in ROM) and directly access video memory to speed up writing to the display. Windows needs to monitor the hardware input/output ports that applications use for this purpose in order to restore the display after you switch to another application and then back to the first one. This PIF option does not affect computers that use a VGA monitor. Another possible cause of a lost display is insufficient video memory. A program that switches from text to graphics mode might not find enough video memory reserved for its display. Selecting the Retain Video Memory PIF option can solve this problem.

A slow running non-Windows application may be the first sign of a memory crunch. A tell-tale sign of a memory squeeze is the frequent appearance of a disk drive light which indicates that a good deal of swapping is taking place. Chapter 11 explored several strategies you can employ to deal with tight memory. If you still experience unacceptable performance after making those adjustments and you run Windows in 386 Enhanced mode, you can increase the value of the PIF's Foreground Priority option to provide the application with more processor time, and clear the Detect Idle Time option in the PIF.

Windows uses a variety of keyboard key combinations for its own purposes (see Table 12-1). If you press a key combination within an application and some unexpected event takes place, you may need to adjust that application's PIF to reserve certain keystroke combinations. In 386 Enhanced mode, there is also an Application Shortcut Key option that may be the culprit. Similarly, if you press one of the key combinations listed in Table 12-1 and the assigned Windows action does not occur, a running application probably has reserved that combination which makes it unavailable until the application is closed.

*Table 12-1: Key combinations reserved for Windows' use.*

| *Key Combination* | *Function* |
|---|---|
| Ctrl+Esc | Switches to Task List. |
| Alt+Esc | Switches to the next application window or minimized icon, including full-screen programs. |
| Alt+Tab | Switches to the next application window, restoring applications that are running as icons. |
| PrtSc | Copies an image of the screen contents onto the Clipboard. |
| Alt+PrtSc | Copies an image of the active window onto the Clipboard. |

| *Key Combination* | *Function* |
|---|---|
| Alt+F4 | Closes the active application window. |
| Ctrl+F4 | Closes the active document window. |
| F1 | Gets Help and displays the Help Index for the application. |

An inability to capture a screen image onto the Clipboard is a problem that might be caused by a PIF selection of the No Screen Exchange option. An incorrect Video Mode option may also prevent this Clipboard exchange. A final possibility is that the PrtSc or Alt+PrtSc keys have been taken over by another application.

Being unable to leave a running application can be caused by an error within the application. Should this error occur, use Ctrl+C or Ctrl+Break to return to Windows. If you still cannot leave the application, press Ctrl+Esc to bring up the Task Manager and then select End Task. 386 Enhanced mode users can press Alt+Spacebar to open the Control menu to select the Terminate option. Your last recourse if all else fails is the Ctrl+Alt+Del combination that restarts the computer. After using the End Task or Terminate functions, you should always restart the machine to assure that both DOS and Windows are stable.

## Using Windows on a Network

Although most people acquire Windows by buying a copy for their computer, they may not have to if they work in an organization with computers hooked together on a local area network (LAN). A single copy of Windows can be shared by all the computers, often called either *workstations* or *nodes* once they have been attached to a network, that are hooked to the LAN. Windows can be customized to suit the tastes of each workstation's user. Windows running on a network shares some of its files with all the network's nodes, and creates other files that become dedicated to individual workstations and are stored in a personal Windows directory. Windows also works with diskless workstations attached to a LAN.

Windows works with Microsoft LAN Manager, Novell Netware, 3Com (and 3+Open), IBM PC LAN, and Banyan VINES 4.0 networking software. Each of these networks requires a variety of different settings in Windows' WIN.INI and SYSTEM.INI configuration files. The Windows Setup program makes or adjusts most of these settings automatically upon installation. Windows may work with other networks, but its features are not guaranteed to function properly.

### Network Users

If your workgroup uses a LAN, your network administrator will let you know when Windows has been installed on the network (see the later section, "Network Administrators" for more about putting Windows on the network). Once Windows is on the network, users of every attached workstation can connect to the network disk and directory where Windows is located and install the shared copy of Windows on their computer. To install Windows from the network, a user starts the Setup program with the "/n" switch at the DOS prompt. Once Setup begins, the installation procedure is very similar to that for the non-network version of Windows.

A key difference between network installation and single-user installation is the requirement for specifying a personal Windows directory. For diskless workstations, this directory will have to reside on a network disk drive. For computers that have their own disks, this special directory should be placed on any hard disk that provides a substantial amount of free disk space.

Each workstation user must follow a few simple rules when using Windows on a network, including:

- Make sure all network software loads into your computer before you load Windows. The best way to make sure that network and other device driver software loads at the right time is to carefully set up the AUTOEXEC.BAT and CONFIG.SYS files.

- Use the same printer port to connect to a network printer. Using a different printer port may cause the incorrect settings to be used for the new printer. Adjusting the Control Panel Printers dialog first will allow you to use a different port with a particular printer.
- Use the same letter designation for the network disk drive each time you start Windows. Because Windows stores the path to the shared Windows directory using the drive letter you use the first time you run Windows, using a different drive letter subsequently will prevent Windows from running.

Once a networked computer has Windows up and running, it can take advantage of the features of Windows to make interacting with both the computer and the network easier. The Windows File Manager provides the same kind of easy file management across network drives as it does for physical disk drives. A Control Panel dialog becomes available to streamline the altering of passwords and other network tasks. The Windows Print Manager offers features for using one or more printers attached to the network.

### Network Administrators

Installing Windows on a network requires a few more steps than for a stand-alone machine. Because the Windows distribution disks store files in compressed format, the EXPAND.EXE program must be used to decompress the files. You can create a batch file that uses the EXPAND.EXE program to copy the Windows files from the distribution disks to a network drive. Figure 12-2 shows the Notepad accessory and one version of this batch file's contents. After creating this batch file (with the name "netload.bat" for example), you next need to copy the EXPAND.EXE utility from the Windows' distribution disk to the network disk.

To use NETLOAD.BAT, you then only need to supply source and destination disk and directory names. For example, the command line

```
netload a:*.* w:\windows
```

tells the batch file to use the disk drive/directory name "a:*.*" as the source and "w:\windows" as the destination for its operation. The batch file will then decompress and copy all the files on the disk in drive A: to the network drive and directory W:\WINDOWS. The batch file should be used to copy each Windows distribution disk.

*Figure 12-2: Notepad and a batch file.*

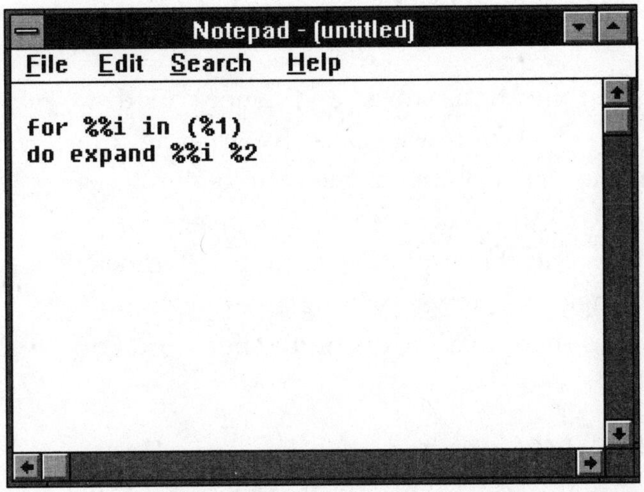


Once the Windows files are stored on the network disk drive, the system administrator needs to rename all the files that have a .SY$ extension so that the extension is .SYS. For example, at the DOS prompt on the network drive the command line

```
rename *.sy$ *.sys
```

will change all the extension of all files from .SY$ to .SYS. Once these files have been renamed, the administrator can load Windows on his or her workstation with the command

```
setup /n
```

so that his or her computer can take advantage of Windows.

The administrator's next task will be to make all the files in the shared Windows directory Read-Only. The File Manager's File menu option Change Attributes can effect this change to the entire \WINDOWS directory by choosing the Select All option before moving on to the Change Attributes option.

Finally, the administrator should make certain that the SYSTEM.INI, WIN.INI, and WIN.COM files do not reside in the shared Windows directory. These files, which are created by Setup when each workstation on the network installs Windows, appear in the personal Windows directory of each user.

System administrators can make applications stored on the network disk drive immediately available to all Windows users by placing the application's name in a special file that remains in the shared Windows directory. This file, called SETUP.INF, has a section labeled *[progman.groups]* which lists the groups and the applications that will appear in a user's various Program Manager windows. Adding an application's name to any of these lists provides them to all users on the network. For example, adding the line

```
"Microsoft Word",f:\word\word.exe
```

to the proper area of SETUP.INF makes the Microsoft Word program appear in every network user's Program Manager Windows Applications group window. System administrators can also add program names to the *[net]* section of SETUP.INF to instruct the Windows Setup program to copy those programs to a user's personal Windows directory when Windows is installed.

### Network Complexities

Networks are often so complex that they make DOS seem simple by comparison. The number of variables that can affect the way a computer or an application runs increases substantially when a network is added to the overall mix of PC hardware and software. Most users cannot be expected to understand how all the disparate parts go together. Any networked workgroup will have one or more human "experts" on staff who will be available to solve any problems that arise. These experts will have a thorough understanding of the network's idiosyncrasies and the variables that affect how the network software gets along with DOS and other software. Nevertheless, there are a few steps you can take if you start having trouble running Windows on a computer attached to a network.

For example, if you have trouble connecting your workstation to network printers or disks from within Windows, make those connections before you start it. Windows also might fail to run a non-Windows application that directly accesses the network. Running Windows in Real mode may be the solution to this problem. Another solution may be to make sure no other programs are running in the background.

If your computer will not run Windows in Standard or 386 Enhanced mode, try to start it in Real mode. Because some network drivers locate themselves in the part of memory between 640K and 1 megabyte, which Windows ordinarily uses when operating in Standard/386 Enhanced mode, you might have to restrict Windows to Real mode operation, or adjust how it uses memory. If Windows runs in Standard mode but not in 386 Enhanced mode, you may need to alter the SYSTEM.INI setting for NetDMASize or add an EMMExclude setting to keep Windows from using certain portions of memory. The network administrator or the network user manual can supply information for these settings.

Windows adds several text files to your hard disk when you install it. These files contain documentation about system-level configurations for Windows. The documentation file SYSINI.TXT explains many of the settings in the SYSTEM.INI file, including network-specific settings. Another file, NETWORKS.TXT, provides additional settings information for particular brands of networking software.

## Summary

Merging Windows into your DOS-based computer environment provides the ultimate combination of power and convenience. Using the tools you have always depended upon, augmented by the new capabilities of Windows, your computer functions at an increased level of sophistication.

TSRs, batch files, and third-party hardware drivers work with Windows in much the same way as with DOS. Network software also coexists with Windows as peacefully as it does with DOS.

When trouble strikes, there are a number of strategies you can employ to get DOS, Windows, and your applications working in harmony. With all the pieces fitted together properly, your computing world can take a giant step toward making your work more productive and enjoyable.

# Index

## D